Discovering Nor

Discovering
Northumberland

RON & MARLENE FREETHY

JOHN DONALD PUBLISHERS LTD
EDINBURGH

ISBN 0 85976 359 5

British Library Cataloguing in Publication Data
A catalogue record for this book is available from
the British Library.

Phototypeset by The Midlands Book Typesetting Company,
Loughborough.
Printed & bound in Great Britain by J. W. Arrowsmith Ltd., Bristol.

Introduction

It is not possible to write a book of this nature without relying on the help of a number of people especially the staff of the many local Tourist Information Offices. We found a friendly welcome everywhere.

During the production of several television films on the area we were helped by many friendly locals. We thank Mr and Mrs Selby Allen for taking the time to explain their sea-life centre at Seahouses, to Freddie the Dolphin for allowing us to swim with him and to Anthony Murray the Master of the cruise boat *Osprey* which operates around Kielder Water. We have a special thanks to Anthony who swiftly overcame our distaste of conifer forests by pointing out the delights of the area from the deck of his craft. We also thank Northumbrian Water for their hospitality whilst discovering Kielder. To Dudley Green who has written *Discovering Hadrian's Wall* we give thanks for companionship whilst exploring the border regions. Our final thanks goes to the county itself which has more hidden and undiscovered spots than anywhere else in England.

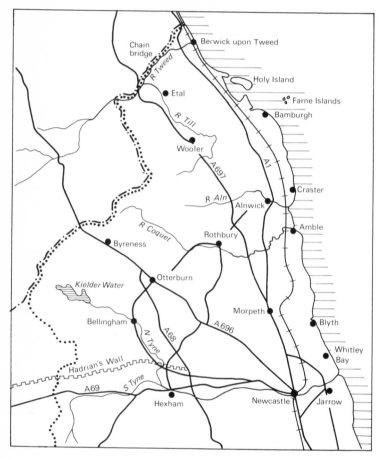

Location Map

Contents

CHAPTER 1

An Introduction to Northumberland

Two events, one family based and the other of a literary nature, stimulated our love and appreciation of Northumberland. In the last years of the 19th century one of our grandfathers and several of our uncles worked in the shipyards of Barrow-in-Furness, then owned by Vickers-Armstrong. All the family knew that the might of the armaments industry which helped in the defeat of first the Kaiser and then Hitler had its origins in and around Tyneside. Barrow was a proud offshoot of the inventions of Armstrong and one of our grandmothers never lost the Northumbrian twang or her love of the old county. She must have spun in her grave when the boundary changes of 1974 effectively removed the counties of Durham and Northumberland and left us with Cleveland and Tyne and Wear. She would never have accepted these new-fangled names and for the purpose of this book on Northumberland, neither do we.

The second event is a much more unusual, and indeed lucky, link. Many years ago we bought a house on the side of Pendle Hill in Lancashire and began to collect as much information as we could concerning the area. We bought a collection of books written by Harrison Ainsworth (1805–82), the Manchester born author who during his lifetime was more successful than Dickens. We bought the collection because it contained the *Lancashire Witches*, a story set around Pendle Hill, but we then began to read the others including *Rookwood* the story of Dick Turpin, and most importantly in the context of this book a rather dated novel called *Preston Fight*. This tells the tragic story of the Earl of Derwentwater although Ainsworth, as he always did, embroidered the story to suit the needs of his fictional work. We followed his story of the *Lancashire Witches* literally on the ground and once this had been done our Northumbrian roots began to drag us in a north-easterly direction to discover the truth concerning one of the county's most loveable yet so tragic figures. This added to our delight in

1

In a county noted for its magnificent castles, Bamburgh is one of the most historic and beautifully situated. It is also in a fine state of repair.

the county and ultimately led many years later, to the writing of this book.

> Farewell to pleasant Dilston Hall
> My fathers ancient seat;
> A stranger now must call thee his,
> Which gars my heart to greet.

Thus wrote Surtees in his poem 'Derwentwater's Farewell' in praise of the popular James Ratcliffe the earl of Derwentwater known throughout Tynedale as 'The Bonnie Earl'. Alas events overtook the unfortunate young man who perished whilst still in the flush of youth by having the misfortune to be cast into the couldron of 17th- and early 18th-century politics. Born in 1689, the first of a family of four in an unhappy marriage, James was heir to vast lands accumulated as befitted a grandson of Charles II. His mother was Lady Mary Tudor who had royal blood in her veins, the result of a liaison between Charles and the actress Moll Davis. Nell Gwyn was not the only mistress that the King did not allow to starve! This Stuart blood pulsing through his veins decided where his support should lie during the Jacobite rebellion of 1715.

2

James was born in London but sent to France to be educated at the court of the exiled Stuarts, and he got to know James Francis who is now known to history as the Old Pretender. Young Derwentwater was both physically and intellectually attractive and even his enemies admired him. The Vicar of Allendale (see Chapter 2), who was chaplain to the Jacobites during the rebellion but who later turned King's evidence to save his own skin, has nothing but good to say of the Earl. In his *History of the Rebellion* he wrote

> The sweetness of his temper and disposition, in which few had equals, had secured him the affection of all his tenants, neighbours and dependants, that multitudes would have lived and died for him; he was a man formed by nature to be generally loved, and he had a benificence so universal that he seemed to live for others ... He kept a house of generous hospitality and noble entertainment which few in that county do and none came up to. He was very charitable to poor and distressed families on all occasions, whether known to him or not, and whether Papist or Protestant.

If this is the written testimony of one who betrayed him and recorded his thoughts in an anti-Jacobite climate we can only imagine what the young Earl's true friends thought of him.

In 1710 the 21-year-old Earl of Derwentwater deemed it safe to return home and take over the running of the family estate at Dilston, which up to that point he had not seen. In five short years he learned to love the place and his workers developed a fierce loyalty towards him which was to cost many of them their own lives. Many local families, also Stuart sympathising Catholics, homed in on Dilston from all over the county and these included the Fenwicks, Erringtons, Collingwoods, Shaftoes, Widdringtons and in particular Tom and Dorothy Forster from Bamburgh. The latter were brother and sister whose exploits during the 1715 rebellion have been every bit as well documented as those of the Earl himself. Tom Forster, in contrast to the Earl, was a hard drinking broad speaking tactless but pleasant tough guy. Tom and Dorothy must have enjoyed the hospitality of Dilston. Earl James rode around his estates with his hot headed young brother Charles and envisaged a plan to rebuild Dilston. By looking at contemporary accounts it would seem that he spent some time at Blanchland (see Chapter 2) in the company of Dorothy Forster, but there does not seem to have been any romantic link between them. Meanwhile the foundations of Dilston were laid and Dilston looked like becoming one of the grandest houses in the county, an enterprise which almost demanded that the Earl should be married. He fortunately met Anna Webb from Dorset and on 10 July 1712 the pair were married. By a strange demand of Anna's father the pair were obliged to spend two years at Hatherhope, the property of the Webb family, but in 1714 they were able to return to Dilston. This year saw the death of Queen Anne which brought the country into the fateful chaos which was to be a tragedy for the young Derwentwaters. Historians have often blamed young Anna for insisting that the Earl should support the Stuarts against the Hanoverians. We feel obliged to ask what alternative the Earl had, having been brought up in France, and especially as James's claim to the throne was stronger than anyone else's. James had one drawback; he was a Catholic, but then so was the Earl of Derwentwater, and this alone may have pursuaded him to join in the rebellion. Certainly the country was thrown into utter confusion, and France was a hotbed of activity. 'The King Over the Water' was the toast of Northumbria and the Earl left the Countess and her baby son on 1 August 1714 as he knew that as soon as the Queen died his life was in danger. He had many friends who willingly gave him shelter despite the threat to their own lives. As a rebellion became ever more certain the Earl of Derwentwater was an obvious choice as a general of the Stuart forces. Then politics took over, as it was thought that Tom Forster would be a better choice, since he was a Protestant who could bring in any Northumbrians who were wavering whether or not to support a Catholic. In the end this was a fateful choice as the hard-drinking, slow-thinking Tom made crucial errors and the brave army which left Rothbury in Coquetdale, their white cockades fluttering proudly in the wind, ground to a comprehensive halt and ignominious defeat at Preston in Lancashire. They marched via Warkworth, Alnwick and Morpeth, picking up troops on the way, but were obliged to bypass Newcastle which had declared itself for the Hanoverians which must have been a bitter disappointment to the Stuarts. Following their march via Kelso and through the Pennines to

The fortified bridge at Warkworth over which Tom Forster's troops must have clattered on their way to defeat in the 1715 rebellion.

Kendal the army approached Preston in November where the ill-disciplined and badly led forces were no match for the well organised Government troops. After a one-sided battle Tom Forster surrendered without conditions and without telling his brother officers. Government retributions were swift and merciless and the leaders, including the Earl of Derwentwater, were taken with their hands bound behind their backs to the Tower of London. The trials were a farce and a foregone conclusion and despite her plea direct to George I young Anna could not prevent the execution of her husband. On 24 February 1716, dressed in black velvet, James the Earl of Derwentwater, climbed the steps up to the scaffold on Tower Hill and his head was chopped from his body. He could have been pardoned if he had renounced his Catholic faith, but he refused. He was 27 years old! Dilston was never completed and the site is said to be haunted by Anna's ghost, the sad lady clutching her fan which she is said to have thrown at the feet of her young husband in an effort to make him take up his sword on behalf of the Stuarts.

Some of the leaders did manage to escape, including Tom Forster and the Earl's brother, Charles Radcliffe. Dorothy Forster travelled south from Northumberland for the first time, bribed a gaoler at Newgate and found a sea captain to take her brother to France. She spread the rumour that Tom had died and an empty coffin was placed in the family vault in Bamburgh church. The coffin bears two dates the last recording 1738 the year of his actual death, following which Tom's body was brought home. Dorothy married a blacksmith from Warenford but when she died in 1771 she was interred next to Tom, although under her married name of Dorothy Armstrong. Charles Radcliffe also escaped from Newgate and made his way to France where he married the Countess of Newburgh. His Stuart sympathies remained and he returned with the Young Pretender in 1745. He was captured again and this time there was no escape. Like his brother he was beheaded. On 8 December 1746 on Tower Hill he died, the last Englishman to be executed by the axe.

The tragic tale of the Earl of Northumberland was, however, not yet over. The body of the Earl was returned to Dilston although his estate was given to the Commissioners of Greenwich hospital. His wife died in Belgium and their son died in a riding accident. There was, however, a second child — a daughter who was born after her father's execution. She married Lord Petré and this family retained many relics from the all but extinct Derwentwater line. In 1805 the vault was opened and a local blacksmith extracted some teeth from the skull and sold them as relics. The pathetic remains were finally taken to the Petré home at Thornton Hall in Essex and laid to rest in 1874. We feel sure that although his body has left Northumberland his soul still remains in its countryside. He would have known the haunting call of the curlew which is now fittingly used as the symbol of the Northumbria National Park.

Far too many people do not think beyond Newcastle and imagine Northumberland as an industrial wasteland. A holiday in this area does not seem a good idea at all. The truth is quite the reverse. Here is a combination of history and natural history, and apart from Newcastle the area is the least populated of any county, with vast areas of open country interspersed with small county towns, delightful villages and magnificent castles — an indication of the military tradition essential for an area on the border between the once separate kingdoms of England and Scotland. The northern coastline is beautiful and unpolluted, with Lindisfarne the cradle of Christianity. On this holy place two opposing views of Christianity met head on. The fiercely aggressive Celts, used to fighting the pagans, merged with the more gentle missionary approach of holy men from the South, and between them they created the Golden Age of Northumbria culminating in the Lindisfarne Gospels and the work of the Venerable Bede. It was in the kingdom of Northumbria therefore that civilisation developed, only to be snuffed out by the Viking attacks beginning in the late eighth century but revived as the Normans established a permanent hold and built their huge stone castles and allowed impressive abbeys to be constructed. All this and the rich natural history make the discovery of Northumberland a delightful combination of industry and insects, buildings, boats and birds, monuments and mammals, flowers, folklore and forts, old coal mines and even older castles. All this and a road system remarkably free from traffic apart from at the peak of the holiday season. Except for Newcastle that is!

CHAPTER 2

The Southern Border

The southern border of Northumberland can be explored by strolling along the banks of four rivers; the East and West Allens which together make up Allendale plus the South and North Tynes. The first three of these rivers are described in this chapter whilst the North Tyne is the subject of Chapter 4. The two Tynes join near Hexham and then flow on to Newcastle, which is described in Chapter 3.

Allendale is now walking country with both rivers fed by many peaty burns which crash down from the uplands. This was never fighting country in the military sense, but for many years it was working country dominated by productive lead mines belonging to the Beaumont family who were the Earls of Allendale. The lead mines began to decline in 1861 and none are now working but there are many chimneys and other reminders of its mineral history. The capital of the area is Allendale Town, now an increasingly popular holiday resort which has a longer season than most. It is usually impossible to find a hotel room on New Year's Eve and parking at this time is always a problem. The Allendale Baal fire originated in pagan times and men known as 'guisers' dress up in peculiar costumes and blacken their faces before parading through the town carrying barrels of blazing tar. This custom may well have been brought to the area by the Norsemen and in the Shetlands it is also the chief guiser who brings in the new year although here they keep to the old style New Year's Day. The celebrations at Allendale go on all night and here the custom of first footing is still seriously maintained. We cannot bring ourselves to ignore it either and as taught by our grandparents we stand outside the house from around five to midnight until we hear the church bells ringing in the New Year. In we then go complete with a piece of coal, a sprinkling of salt and some money to be greeted by a glass of something strong and warming. A dark man should, according to tradition, enter first, and as neither of us qualify we allow our black labrador to come with us! The

"Guising" at Allendale on New Years Eve.

tradition of a dark first footer obviously relates to the guisers with their blackened faces.

The scenery around Allendale is wild and wonderful, the town itself being 1,400 feet (427 metres) above sea level and it claims to be the precise geographical centre of the British Isles. It was certainly the centre of the lead mining industry with almost 20 per cent of Britain's output being produced around Allendale. The Quakers were very much involved in the development of lead mining and Allendale had many followers of this faith. The parish church, however, also has an interesting tale to tell. The origin of St Cuthbert's may well be Norman but the present building was only consecrated in 1873. The chapel of Our Lady of Allendale was given to the Prior of Hexham in 1174 but a new church was built in the fourteenth century. There were further rebuildings in 1807 and 1873 but nobody seems to know why the dedication was changed to St Cuthbert. The Vicar of Allendale in the early eighteenth century was named Patten, the chaplain to the Stuart troops of the 1715 rebellion and who turned King's Evidence after the defeat as mentioned in the last chapter.

The head of the East Allen river is appropriately called Allenheads and it was here that most of the profitable lead mines were situated. Prior to the exploitation of lead the area was preserved as a hunting area which meant a sparse population and few farms. This meant no castles, no battles, no border raiders and plenty of peace below the 2,000 feet (609 metres) peak of Kilhope Law from which the East Allen crashes down towards Allendale town. The upper reaches of the West Allen are also pretty wild and the first settlement to be reached is the attractive little hamlet of Ninebanks. The only building of note here is a four-storeyed tower, which does not appear dominant because the ground around it has been raised so much that the original slit of the basement is now almost level with the road. A Jacobean newel staircase was built at the same time as the fourth storey. Close to the hamlet at Old Town the waters of the two Allen rivers meet and there are a few remains of buildings here which possibly account for the name of Old Town. Below Ninebanks the scenery is beautiful with the wooded valley overlooked by the mass of Whitfield Fell; Whitfield itself is a pretty spot and has two churches. The old church is tucked away off the main road but the new church is nearer the settlement and was built by Mrs Blackett-Ord in memory of her uncle, and it was dedicated in 1860. The Ord family lived at Whitfield Hall which is situated about one mile to the south on the bank of the river. It was built during the reign of Henry VI (1422–1461) but was enlarged substantially in the 17th century. At this time the estate was owned by the Whitfield family but in the mid 18th century they found themselves in severe financial difficulties and the estate was sold to William Ord of Fenham who employed Newton, a Newcastle architect, to rebuild the house in 1785. A further storey was added in 1856. The Ord family made substantial improvements to the area including the financing of the 1778 turnpike road and its improvement in 1824. They allowed the road to pass through more than seven miles of the estate. The improved communications enabled the lead mines owned by the London lead company to flourish. Near the junction of the East and West Allen rivers the company built a reverbatory smelting furnace called Cupola Mills. Although the furnaces have gone the name remains at Cupola bridge, now a delightful spot from which to view the Allen.

On its way down to the Tyne the Allen flows through a number of beauty spots including a deep pool known as Cypher's Linn which legend says has a treasure in gold lying in the bottomless pool. It is alleged that a party of monks submerged their coffers to keep them from raiders. The story continues as it is also suggested that a local farmer sank a hook and caught the treasure. It does not say if an endless rope was used to reach the bottomless pit! He attached the other end of the rope to a team of oxen but when they began to pull they were dragged into the river and never seen again, and neither was the farmer who greedily held on to the rope. In the last century a fisherman either with an imagination, or a sense of humour, reported during a spell of very dry weather the horns of an ox just visible below the surface of the Linn. There are many riverside walks along the Allen including the area known as Raven's Crag which spectacularly overhangs a deep pool, the whole area being given to the National Trust by the Hon. Francis Bowes-Lyon, an uncle of the Queen Mother. The river is crossed by a number of rope bridges which sway in the wind and vibrate with the footsteps of those trying to cross, and nearby is the ruin of Staward Pele, once one of the important military defences in the area. The Carts Bog Inn is a good place to enjoy a bar snack. There is a good car park at Plandy Mill. Here is the ideal spot to watch goosander and common sandpiper both of which breed along the riverbank and Ridley Woods are at their best in spring when bluebells bloom and the heronry is in full swing as the breeding season reaches its climax with young birds standing on their huge nests high in the trees demanding to be fed. We were once lucky enough to be able to watch a kingfisher dive from the branch of an alder tree and splash into the river only to emerge

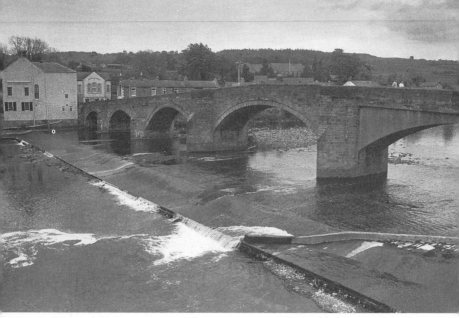

Haydon Bridge is one of the most beautiful bridges spanning the South Tyne river, but is now restricted to pedestrians.

seconds later with a bullhead in its bill. It returned to its perch and droplets of water glistened as the sunlight fell on its oily plumage.

The scenery around the upper reaches of the South Tyne is equally impressive and continues to fascinate the naturalist all the way down to its junction with the North Tyne at Hexham and beyond. Rising on the slopes of Cross Fell in Cumbria the South Tyne is one of the few Northumbrian streams which rises beyond the boundaries of the county.

Haydon Bridge is the perfect base from which to explore the source of the South Tyne by following it upstream. This village straddles the A69 Carlisle to Newcastle road and the bridge from which it takes its name was vital to both the Scots and English armies. This accounts for the fact that the bridge was once gated so that it could be locked against the Scottish invaders. There was a bridge here from medieval times but it was destroyed in the floods of 1773 and was replaced by the present graceful span. This is now only used by pedestrians with traffic carried on a new rather ugly bridge a little distance downstream. On a bank of the river is Haydon

12

The common sandpiper is a summer visitor arriving in April to breed along the banks of Northumbrian rivers including the South Tyne.

Spa, a medicinal spring which almost, but not quite, allowed the village to develop into a health resort. Haydon old church stands forlornly on a hillside and is thought to have been one of the many places where the followers carrying the remains of St Cuthbert to keep them from the invading Danes, rested awhile.

The old church is said to date to around 1190, although alterations, including the chantry, were added in the 14th century. The chapel in the south wall is particularly interesting as is the font which was fashioned from a Roman altar probably brought from a site near the Roman Wall. Some essential restoration work was carried out in 1882 by C. C. Hodges. The key can be obtained from the vicarage of St Cuthberts church almost half a mile to the south in the village itself. The parish church was consecrated in 1796 on land given by Greenwich hospital. This provides an interesting connection with the Earl of Derwentwater whose estates were given to the hospital following his execution. The ill-fated Earl also owned Langley Castle a medieval stronghold built in 1360 and which has been restored, although substantially altered, and is now a well appointed hotel. Another local man, enjoyed a much happier life than the Earl was the artist John Martin who was born in 1789 in a little two-roomed cottage at East Land Ends Farm. They say that a prophet is recognised everywhere except in his own country and the same often applies to artists. His most famous picture *The Plains of Heaven* is said to depict his native valley, and long before the young boy could afford the proper material he is said to have drawn pictures in the sandy bays of the South Tyne and also painted in oils on calico. He was apprenticed to a coach-builder in Newcastle, but had much more ambition than just to decorate vehicles. He became a pupil of Boniface Musso and when he left for London he took Martin with him. John specialised in painting scenes from the Old Testament and his canvas *Belshazzar's Feast* won a £200 prize from the British Institution. John Martin also worked as an engraver and was so well regarded that his *Illustrations of Milton* commanded the then enormous sum of 2,000 guineas. His work seems to have been known everywhere except in his native Haydon Bridge. He wrote to the secretary of the local reading room offering to provide the committee with copies of all his famous works. The secretary did not even feel that the offer was worth bringing to the notice of the members! In 1854, some years later, the letter came to light and the offer was finally accepted, the reply reaching John on the Isle of Man on the very day of his death. The only memorial to the life of a quite remarkable artist in his home village is in the name John Martin Street. He attended the Grammar School founded in 1685 as a result of the Shafto Trust, money given by a member of the famous family:

> Bobbie Shafto's gone to sea,
> Silver buckles on his knee
> He'll come back and marry me
> Bonnie Bobbie Shafto.

To the north west of Haydon bridge is Chesterwood, yet another hamlet having associations with the Earl of Derwent-water. Frank Stokoe lived at the Pele tower in the village and he was one of the few who escaped unscathed from the Preston Fight and he was also one of the men who helped to bring the Earl's body back to Dilston.

Although Newcastle is our favourite place from which to explore Hadrian's Wall, Haltwhistle on the South Tyne does have a valid claim as an ideal focus and is worth exploration in its own right. It has a well stocked if small Information Centre next to a car park which also serves the leisure centre and swimming pool. The area is well signed from the town centre which consists of a ribbon of grey shops and houses which straddle the A69 running from Newcastle to Carlisle. The derivation of the name Haltwhistle is likely to remain a mystery for ever and the locals pronounce it Hautwessel. Some suggest it means 'The High Watch Hill' which obviously means a beacon, whilst others think it derives from the 'Holy Hill of the High Water'. The town suffered badly during the border raids and the powerful Ridley family were much feared at this time. In the church of the Holy Cross is the tombstone of John Ridley, the brother-in-law of the Protestant martyr, Nicholas Ridley, the Bishop of London, who along with Bishop Latimer was burned at the stake in 1555 on the orders of Bloody Mary Tudor as she strove to restore the Old Religion following her father's rejection of the Papacy. Holy Cross is one of the most important and interesting churches in Northumberland built in Saxon times on a site probably associated with the Saints Aidan and Paulinus. The present church is largely 13th century, but sensibly restored around 1870, a period not normally noted for retaining the good points of original architecture. The east window is a 13th-century triplet of lancets and these blend surprisingly well with the 19th-century stained glass, a fine example of the work of William Morris. Inside the church is a 7th-century water stoup said to have been used by Paulinus, a memorial stone to Ridley, and grave effiges associated with the local families of Blenkinsopp and Thirlwell.

To the north-west of Haltwhistle is the Roman Wall which we describe in the next chapter, whilst the South Tyne leads in the opposite direction into the Pennines. At one time the South Tyne railway ran from Haltwhistle to Alston in Cumbria but this route was closed in 1976, more than 120 years after its opening by the Newcastle and Carlisle railway. Since 1984 part of the narrow gauge railway has run out of Alston as a tourist attraction but alas it does not now reach Haltwhistle, and South Tynedale is robbed of a once vital rail link with Newcastle and Carlisle. The area can, however, be explored by car and if time permits even more excitingly and profitably on foot. Two interesting buildings in the area are Bellister Castle and Featherstone Castle. Bellister is a ruined pele more or less in the centre of the estate of 1,100 acres (445 hectares) administered by the National Trust. The pele can be visited by permission of the tenant. The castle stands on a rocky eminence which was one time surrounded by a substantial moat. The Blenkinsopp family obtained permission to crenellate their home in 1339 and were still the owners in 1470 and the ruins of their pele was incorporated into a 17th-century house which was altered in the early 19th century. There is rather a grizzly ghost story concerning Bellister and its Grey Man which has more than a hint of a Sherlock Holmes story about it. It tells of an innocent wandering ministrel who called at the hall of the Blenkinsopp's and begged shelter. After granting the poor man's request the Lord became suspicious that the minstrel was actually a spy in disguise and must have made his feelings obvious. The minstrel fled and the Lord, assuming that this was an admission of guilt, loosed his bloodhounds which tore the minstrel to pieces after cornering him on the banks of the South Tyne. The ghost of the victim is said to have haunted the area ever since.

Featherstone Castle, three miles south west of Haltwhistle also has its ghost or rather a whole collection of them! Few castles were more delightfully positioned than this, set at the confluence of the South Tyne and its tributary the Hartley Burn. Helias de Featherstonhaugh was in residence in the area prior to 1212, the manor at that time being under Scottish rule and part of the barony of Langley. Experts have dated part of Featherstone Castle to be earlier than 1200. Around 1300 Thomas de Featherstonehaugh had great power in the area, being guardian of Hexham, Wark and the baronry of Tindale. Such a man certainly required a fortified residence and the L-shaped tower was built. The Featherstonehaughs lost their estates during the Civil Wars, as did many of the Northumbrian gentry, after backing the defeated and executed Charles I against his parliament. The estate was sold to the Earl of Carlisle but in 1711 a descendant who had become Lord Mayor of London bought back the estate. When his son inherited the castle he preferred to stay on his estate in Sussex and sold Featherstone Castle to James Wallace whose descendants changed their name to Hope-Wallace and this family retained ownership until it became a school during the Second World War. It is now one of the most interesting hotels to be found in the country. Wandering around the older portions of the house and the grounds it is easy to imagine the influential Featherstonehaugh family, including Richard who was chaplain to Catherine of Aragon and who remained so loyal to the first wife of Henry VIII that he was executed for speaking out against the King's marriage to Anne Boleyn. A ghost story associated with the castle has its origins in the long-standing feud between the Featherstonehaughs and the Ridleys brought to a head when the heiress Abigail fell in love with a Ridley. Her father forced her to marry Timothy who was her distant cousin. Part of the wedding festivities was to hold a ritual hunt, and during this event Abigail's group was ambushed by the Ridleys and many of the bridal party were killed, including the bride who tried to place herself between her new husband and her lover. The Ridley, seeing what had happened, killed himself and the ghosts of the party are now said to haunt the grounds.

Before reaching the source of the South Tyne three more interesting hamlets are worth exploring, although they are seldom listed in guide books. Lambley is just south of the confluence of the Blackburn with the South Tyne and this is mentioned in 1201 as the site of a small convent of Benedictine Nuns. In 1296 the Scots burned the house but the nuns returned and restored the building which was dissolved in 1538 on the orders of Henry VIII by which time its annual income was £5 15s. 8d. Six nuns were in residence on the date of Dissolution. No sign now remains of the convent as the ruins were long since swept away by the flood waters of the South Tyne. The church at Lambley is dedicated to St Mary and St Patrick. It was built in 1885 and designed by William Searle Hicks, but it has little to commend it architecturally. There is, however, one structure of architectural merit at Langley in the form of the railway viaduct soaring 110 feet (33.5 metres) above the South Tyne. This is certainly one of the finest monuments to the Railway Age.

Kirkhaugh should not be regarded as a village or even as a hamlet. It is merely a dispersed collection of farms with the church at the focus. It was only dedicated in 1869 but it replaced a ruinous medieval church, both being dedicated to the Holy Paraclete — the only buildings in England to be so named. A chalice dated 1571 is a reminder of the old church and the Saxon cross in the churchyard is proof that there has been a religious focus here for very much longer. The church stands in the middle of a field, in a delightfully attractive area not far from the hamlet of Slaggyford which is overlooked by Williamstone Fell and close to the South Tyne river. This clatters over its stony bed and which accounts for the name of Slaggy Ford.

A really substantial village on the southern border is Blanchland, and although it has been described as a picture-postcard village, we think it is far too real for that. Its attractions are in its solid strength and its sudden appearance at the foot of a hill, round a corner and over a bridge across the River Derwent after a journey over the Pennine Hills from Staindrop, Stanhope and Edmundbyers in Durham. The village and the nearby Derwent Reservoir actually straddle the border between County Durham and Northumberland. The village was actually planned by the Trustees of the Lord Crewe estate to provide housing for the lead miners of the area, but the construction was carried out in the best possible taste around the foundations of Blanchland abbey, one-time home of the White monks who owned the land and which gave the village its name. There are three very solid reminders of the abbey — the gatehouse, the Lord Crewe Arms and what is now the parish church. The abbey itself was built in the 12th century but the massive gatehouse dates to the 15th century, the entrance of which now leads into the village square. The building itself now houses the post office which is also a well-stocked general store, selling books and maps as well as the usual essential provisions. Its main exterior feature is the white painted Victorian post box. The Lord Crewe Arms was once the abbey guest house named after the former Bishop of Durham who owned the building after the Dissolution. There are few more interesting hotels than this and we love to have a quiet drink in the garden which was once the abbey cloister. The abbey itself was established on ground given by Walter de Bolbee to a group of Premonstratensian canons who later amalgamated with the Cistercians. Although the abbey church has been much altered since the abbey was dissolved by Henry VIII there are still a few obvious connections with the past. The present church is actually the 13th-century chancel of the once much larger abbey church and there are three medieval coffin lids in the transept, two of which celebrated the lives of abbots; the third was of Robert de Egylston who was the abbey's huntsman. The hunting connection continued after the Dissolution when, after a period in the hands of the Radcliffes, it was bought in 1623 by the Forsters who also owned Bamburgh and who played such a vital role in the life and death of the Earl of Derwentwater. The Forsters probably used Blanchland as a basis for their hunting trips and the Abbot's House as their lodge. In 1699 a Dorothy Forster married Lord Crewe who bought the Blanchland estate, which was heavily burdened by debts, in 1704. It was Lord Crewe's niece, the second Dorothy Forster, who took the prominent role in the 1715 rebellion and who is the central figure in Sir Walter Besant's novel which was named after her. Many scenes were set at Blanchland and at Bamburgh. The novel tells the story of Dorothy who hid her brother in a priest's hole in the Lord Crewe Arms and her ghost is said to haunt one of the bedrooms and to wander the remote local moorlands. When Lord Crewe died he left the income from his estates to Oxford and to a number of schools and almshouses. It was money from this which allowed the present village to be planned and constructed in the mid 18th century and also funded the restoration of the abbey. Lord Crewe's estate also funded many projects around Bamburgh which will be described in Chapter 9.

Downstream from Blanchland the River Derwent has been dammed to produce the Derwent reservoir. The water is now surrounded by a series of conifer lined walks, there are plenty of picnic areas and some really productive bird-watching areas, one of which has an excellent hide. The fishing is also excellent and on a bright day there are splendid views over the water on which there is plenty of activity due to a large sailing club, and the views of the Pennines are worth travelling many a mile to see.

CHAPTER 3

Around a New Castle and an Old Wall

Newcastle itself has a long and fascinating history, but it is also the cultural and historical focus for the whole of the county of Northumberland. The fact that the politicians removed the city from Northumberland to Tyne and Wear in 1974 is irrelevant. It should bear a label reading 'Discoverers of Northumberland — start here'. A long and exciting stay in the city will allow all the fascinating museums to be visited, but this is best done after reading as many books on its history as possible, or better still to lay out the small fee required to join one of the expertly guided city tours, details of which are available from the Tourist Information Office, the Central Library or on the concourse of the Central Station. The tours run from May to September; the energetic can walk, but for those who prefer to conserve their energy there are very reasonably priced coach tours. We who had listened to our grandparents extoll the virtues of the city and the brilliance of its footballers such as the Robledos, Joe Harvey and Jackie Milburn, knew most of the districts of the city by name — but only by name. Eventually we tramped every street of Newcastle and we now bore our son with tales of glorious Tyneside.

Central station is a real reminder of Victorian grandeur. It was built between 1845 and 1850 — a fine example of the work of John Dobson, being officially opened on 29 August 1850 by Queen Victoria. The eastern portico of the station stands on the site of the stank tower which was an important area of the old town walls. Apart from the station, which was modified in 1860 and 1890, John Dobson also designed the Royal Station hotel which was also opened in 1850 and extended 40 years later. It is fitting that the Stephenson Monument should be close to both the station and the hotel which catered for its customers. The monument was designed by J. G. Lough and erected in 1862. It stands on the site once occupied by the chapel of St Mary the Virgin hospital — it's a pity that both this ancient building and the monument

to Stephenson could not have been allowed to stand side
by side.

As it developed Newcastle had the need of four parish
churches, of which St Nicholas's, now the cathedral, and St
John's are of particular interest. The spire of All Saints' is also
a remarkable structure, but the building itself is now used by an
educational charity called 'Town Teacher'.

To discover what medieval Newcastle looked like, it is best to
find the point where the Tyne is joined by its little tributary
called the Lort Burn. From an area called the Sandhill a
steep street called 'The Side' climbs towards St Nicholas's,
which dates mainly to the mid 14th century, but there are
many indications of earlier work. The tower and the spire
are both 15th century but some alterations were made in the
19th century by Green and Dobson. St John's church is also
mainly 14th and 15th century but with some rather tasteful
rebuilding around 1848. In the churchyard are the graves
of two locally important poets. Edward Chicken wrote 'The
Collier's Wedding' and John Cunningham put pen to paper
in praise of 'Newcastle Beer' and we doubt if he is alone in
his love for the delicious brew. Good beer should be enjoyed in
good old pubs, and down near the quay in the Close is a timber
framed inn called the Cooperage. Many a traditional pub these
days breaks the Trade's Description Act without being aware
of it. They advertise 'real ale' even though this has not been
brewed since the Middle Ages.

Ale was the drink of Old England and was a thick sweet drink
made from malt and rather like barley water in consistency.
Barley malt was said to make the best ale although wheat and
oat malt were also used. Ale had a fault — it soon went sour
and had to be drunk soon after brewing; this meant it could
not be transported very far. Alegar was the name given to sour
ale; it was used in the same way that we now use vinegar and it
was often used in medieval recipes. Beer was a brew favoured
on the continent and was made from malt and hops, both of
which were imported from Holland. This thin brew kept well,
but obviously English brewers did not welcome it and in the
late 15th and early 16th centuries the import of beer and hops
was banned in many towns. Eventually, however, beer killed
off ale and these days we drink our pint rather than chew it.

This photograph taken in the 1930's shows how little care was taken to preserve Newcastle's ancient keep when the Victorian rail network was planned.

Newcastle beer — not ale — is now as strong as any brewed in Europe.

Newcastle originally developed on the slopes of a series of sweeping hills overlooking a loop of the River Tyne and the first settlement arose because it offered the lowest bridgeable point over the Tyne. No doubt the area was settled by the Celts, but it was the Romans who built Pont Aelius close to the position of the present swing bridge. This was guarded by a fort which was an integral part of Hadrian's Wall. Little happened hereabouts during the so-called Dark Ages but the Norman Conquest resulted in a repeat of the dual problem faced by the Romans — how to push a boundary to the north and then hold it. The Normans' answer was not a wall but the construction of a New Castle from which the city has taken its name. Initially this was built by William the Conqueror's natural son and was nothing more than a wooden structure on top of the Roman ruins; the new invaders also restored the bridge, which was operational by the middle of the 12th century. By the time of Henry I (1101–35) Newcastle was already an important trading centre but it seems not to have been granted a market charter at this time; by 1205, when King John ruled England, Newcastle ranked eighth in the export league of English ports. The city developed so rapidly during the 19th century that most of the

This picture of the George V Bridge at Newcastle-upon-Tyne was taken in the 1950's.

ancient buildings were demolished as space was at a premium. It is only when the antiquarian explores Newcastle that it is realised just how much does actually remain. Of the castle there is a very well-preserved keep and the 13th-century fortified Black Gate, the two now separated by a network of railway lines which were pushed through the castle when industrial progress meant more than municipal pride. The High Level bridge closes the circle around the castle, but the view from the roof of the Keep over the River Tyne is startlingly attractive. The Keep also looks at its most impressive when viewed from across the river — and area planted with trees with winding and steep footpaths leading up from the river. The Keep is open throughout the year on payment of a small fee, but the authorities point out that the steep stairs are too difficult for the disabled. Spiral stairs lead to the roof, and rooms on view include the Great Hall, Garrison Room, Queen's Chamber and a truly beautiful Norman chapel. The Keep was built by Robert Curthose, the bastard son of William the Conqueror. The museum is closed only on Mondays and houses a display covering the history of Newcastle. The Black Gate dates to

24

Newcastle has one of the most modern shopping centres in Europe.

the 13th century and is now surmounted by a 17th-century dwelling, said to be named after its first occupant who was called Patrick Black. Close by are the old Barbican walls dating from the 13th century; the Heron Pit prison, although modified in the 17th century, is also of 13th-century origin.

Medieval Newcastle stood as a bastion against the Scots and was thus confined with its two-mile circle of wall, part of which has been restored. The west wall on Bath Lane is worth exploring as is the Plummer Tower on Croft Street which now houses some furnishings from the Laing Art Gallery. The latter has a fine collection of art, glass, ceramics, textiles and silver, and is rightly recognised as the major gallery in the north-east of England. The local authority has also restored the Wall Knowl Tower which was an important Sally Port set on the summit of the Causey Bank Steps. The protection offered by the walled city ensured its development as an important market town and its docks developed because of the close proximity of easily mined coal; indeed Newcastle mines were the first to export the black gold, and its fortunes were largely built upon it. No doubt the plentiful supply of cheap fuel and a sheltered area of deep water led to Newcastle becoming a centre for heavy industry during the 19th century. Good communications need bridges and the High Level Bridge built in 1849 carried road and rail over the Tyne. It is a fine example of the work of Robert Stephenson, son of George. The Swing Bridge is the work of Lord Armstrong who loved, lived in and worked tirelessly in Northumberland. This bridge was built in 1876 as a replacement for the medieval bridge. The main railway bridge, the King Edward, was opened in 1906; also built in the 20th century are the Redheugh and the Tyne road bridges plus of course the tunnel. Around these spans the Quayside Sunday Market adds colour and atmosphere to replace the once thriving industry of the docks. The most recent bridge carries the new Metro out to South Tyneside. This is the city's most rapid transit system and incorporates an underground stretch and a total of 44 stations. The cost of travel on the Metro is competitive and it is one of the best ways of exploring the city since it avoids visitors having to battle with the one-way motorway system which cuts through the centre and with parking which can be difficult, although there are a number of multi-storey parks close to the centre.

Eldon Square is one of the most modern shopping centres created by demolishing an area of Victorian elegance, but however much criticism it has received there are few such areas to compete with it outside London. We have spent several periods in Norway and the boat always seems full of Norwegians who find it cheaper to shop in Newcastle than they do at home. Careful planning and bulk buying, especially for clothes and sports equipment, easily pays for the crossing and provides a healthy profit. It is hard to find a Norwegian in and around Stavanger or Bergen who does not know Eldon Square and has not enjoyed a meal in one of the restaurants or sampled the variety of fast food outlets. Sporting and leisure activities are also on offer and the facilities for babies and children and for the disabled are second to none.

Within easy walking distance of Eldon Square is Grey Street — a real touch of Victorian elegance dominated by

Newcastle, its castle and its bridges viewed from a commercial area of the river.

a monument which is a rival to Nelson's Column. It was erected to commemorate the passing of the Reform Bill of 1832 and this was during the period that Lord Grey was Prime Minister. It is open, to those with enough energy to climb the stairs, on Saturdays and Bank Holidays between Easter and September. The view from the top is magnificent and the layout of the city, especially Grey Street itself, is seen as on a map. The magnificent Theatre Royal, which has a pillared entrance, looks beautiful when illuminated and the building is rightly regarded as the cultural focus of the North East. Nineteenth-century Newcastle was planned and fashioned by the Town Clerk John Clayton, architects Dobson and Oliver and builder Richard Granger. Much of their work remains and very fine it is, but the original Eldon Square was demolished as we have seen to make way for the new shopping centre. Their work was functional as well as decorative and this is very evident in the railway station. This area is ideal to begin an exploration of the Keep Museum.

Apart from the Keep Museum already mentioned, Newcastle has many other museums. The Military Vehicle Museum at the Exhibition Park Pavilion houses a collection gathered by the North Military Vehicle Club. The Pavilion is all that remains of the complex built in 1929 for the North East Coast Exhibition. Behind the attractively pillared entrance is a mass of machinery, equipment and vehicles, most of them dating to the Second World War. The fascinating collection is open daily. The Greek Museum in the Percy Building of the University has a variety of Greek and Etruscan artefacts, especially vases, metalwork, armour and a wide range of terracottas. The Halton Gallery, also part of the University, has a large collection of paintings and drawings. There is always something of interest going on here, be it temporary exhibitions or lunchtime discussions. It is open from Monday to Friday during term time and is run as an integral part of the Classics Department.

Of particular interest to us, and to those who wish to discover Northumberland is the Hancock Museum which was purpose-built in 1878. Again the University plays an active role in the running of this Natural History collection and works in partnership with the Natural History Society of Northumbria. Geological and Natural History specimens are beautifully displayed. John Hancock's bird collection from which the museum takes its name is among the best in the country. Another gallery holds Abel Chapmen's trophies (see Chapter 4) which have been so displayed that they appear to be looking out from the portholes of Noah's Ark. There is also a display of the work of Thomas Bewick who worked in Newcastle but who was born at Cherryburn on the outskirts of the city and which is described later in this chapter.

The museum of Science and Engineering at Blandford House provides a comprehensive history of Tyneside's industrial development. This includes a model set into a wall which shows what the city looked like in 1929 — active, mucky, murky and magnificent! The museum, entry to which is free, is closed on Sundays and Mondays, but on Saturdays free film shows are arranged for children. This is the way municipal pride is nurtured. The Maritime gallery is of particular interest and links well with a visit to the Trinity Maritime Centre on the Quayside. Here in an old Victorian warehouse is a display of maritime history.

The elegant Theatre Royal, Newcastle.

The John George Joicey Museum in the so-called Jesus Hospital on City Road also opens from Tuesday to Saturday and is set in one of Newcastle's most interesting buildings. It is an arcaded 17th-century set of almshouses constructed of brick and with stone mouldings. Here is a collection of illustrative material relating to the city; there is also much military material, including the artefacts of the 15th/19th King's Royal Hussars and the Northumberland Hussars. It is vital that such regiments are remembered, particularly during the 1990s when the raising of the iron curtain has resulted in the slimming down of the armed forces.

The final museum on our list is, in terms of Northumberland in general as opposed to Newcastle in particular, the most important. The University of Newcastle administers the Museum of Antiquities and the basis of its collection was gathered by the Society of Antiquaries of Newcastle upon Tyne. It is closed on Sundays but it must be visited, especially by those fascinated by the Wall. Here is a scale model of the structure and a walk-in set up of a temple to Mithras, plus a very lifelike audiovisual presentation. There are countless artefacts from the prehistoric period to the Middle Ages but the emphasis is not on the New Castle but firmly and quite correctly on the Old Wall.

The Grey monument, Newcastle's rival to Nelson's column.

The Wall is Britain's most famous ancient monument and is thus Northumberland's most important tourist attraction. Many books have been written on it, some of which are mentioned in the Further Reading List. We enjoyed, with Dudley Green, many visits to the Wall both in Cumbria and Northumberland, and we are grateful for Dudley's company and to be able to read his learned book in this series on Hadrian's monument. For us the Wall has provided a focal point from which to launch into a discovery of southern Northumberland. Originally the Wall stretched about 80 Roman miles (76 'modern' miles) from Wallsend, now in Northumberland, and Bowness-on-Solway now in the county of Cumbria. The modern border is at the River Irthing and the Cumbrian stretch of the Wall is described in our companion volumes *Discovering Cumbria* and *Discovering the Pennines.*

The idea was almost certainly conceived by the Emperor Hadrian when he abandoned the attempt to occupy Scotland and decided that the most easily defined border would be between the Tyne and the Solway. Actually the frontier was defined not by one barrier but two — the Wall and a flat-bottomed ditch called 'the vallum' which preceded the Wall and had little if any military significance. The vallum simply indicated the border, although this was patrolled by troops based in one of ten forts, the most westerly of which was at Burgh-on-Sands in Cumbria whilst that furthest to the east was at Benwell. The vallum was not meant to deter whole armies but to discourage smuggling and cross-border raiding. The precise date of the digging of the vallum is not known, but was probably in the early years of Hadrian's reign, perhaps around AD 120. The vallum must only have been partially successful and a decision was made to construct a more formidable barrier — a wall used to police the border — and there was never enough room on top for troops to march. The physical work of construction was given to three legions — the second known as Augusta, the sixth known as Victrix Pia Fidelis and the twentieth the Valeria Victrix. Each century of men, controlled by a centurion was given its own section to build, and the men took such pride in their work that they inscribed the stone of their section, and many of these 'signatures' can still be seen. Originally the wall was to be 17 feet (5.2 metres) high and between 6 and 8 feet (1.8 and 2.4 metres) wide. It was manned by troops based in 17 forts between which at regular intervals were placed the appropriately named mile castles. Actually a Roman mile was equivalent to 540 yards (494 metres). The milecastles themselves were linked by signal towers and thus news was passed along the wall with surprising speed.

Between the Wall and the vallum ran the Roman Military Way known as the Stanegate. Sometimes this is confused with the Military Way planned by General Wade following the uprising of 1745 when troop movements had been difficult. Many miles of Wall and stretches of Stanegate were destroyed to provide materials for this road. The Military Road is still used in part today and links Newcastle to Stanwix near Carlisle and for many miles it passes close to the Wall. Tourists find it ideal and although there are no convenient 'unofficial car parks' there are several museums along the Wall, each of which has car parking, refreshment and toilet facilities.

The Wall began (or should it be 'ended'?) at Wallsend which the Romans called Segedunum and which was sited on the banks of the Tyne some six miles below the bridge of Pons Aelii. As shipbuilding developed on the river no thought was given to Wallsend which disappeared beneath a web of concrete, bricks, cranes and machinery. In the late 18th century colliery buildings stood on the site of the fort itself and much damage was done, although much worse was to follow. For many years Segedunum lay beneath a housing estate. This has now gone, the ruins of the fort have been excavated and a Heritage Centre set up. Close to this is a car park, bus station and Metro station, providing a fast service into Newcastle. The positions of the fort walls and gates have been marked out and within the Heritage Centre is a scale model of the fort in its heyday when it was home to 480 infantry and 120 cavalry, many of whom would have their families with them. There were four gates, three leading out into the open country and the fourth leading to the family settlement situated between the river and the fort and thus protected by the troops. The name Segedunum meant either 'strong fort' or 'victory fort' and the present Heritage Centre is certainly a victory for the conservationists, and archeological investigations are continuing, which makes regular visits equally enjoyable, especially if your trip coincides with one of the frequently organised guided walks. The Fort itself is open all year and access is free, as is the Heritage Centre which is closed on Mondays. From Tuesday to Friday it opens from 10 a.m. to 5.30 p.m. and on Saturdays from 10 a.m. to 5.30 p.m. On Sundays it only opens between Easter and

October from 2 p.m. to 5 p.m. There are good facilities for the disabled.

Although it is strictly off the line of the Wall the South Shields Roman Fort and Museum is worth a visit as it is a 3rd Century AD supply base set back from the Wall, obviously to protect it. Again entry is free with opening times similar to Segedunum, and it also closes on Mondays except for Bank Holidays. The fort is close to the seafront which is rapidly becoming popular with visitors. The real joy of Arbeia, as the fort was known to the Romans, is the accurately reconstructed west gate and the fine museum which has audiovisual displays and lots of artefacts. Again the facilities for the disabled are excellent. There is a car park and a picnic site, and as at Wallsend, excavations are continuing to unravel the history of the fort all of which make us look forward to a return visit.

After passing through Newcastle the next interesting place on the Wall is at Benwell which is maintained by English Heritage; it is open all the time and entry is free. There are no facilities and the site is reached to the south of the A69. It is, however, one of the most fascinating places on the Wall — the Romans knew it as Condercum, and it was a small temple dedicated to the local god Antenociticus. It is possible to delineate the lines of the temple including the base of a statue flanked by altars. The god's bust and two altars are on display at the Museum of Antiquities in Newcastle. Initially there would have been a fort here also but this has long since been swallowed by the urban sprawl, although there is still some evidence of the vallum ditch.

At this point most people on a discovery trip along the Wall head for Corbridge, but there is one little gem which should not be missed, and that is Denton Hall Turret, just to the south of the A69, which was excavated in the late 1980s. Here it can be seen how the vallum was actually cut nearly 7 feet (2 metres) through solid rock. The turret and a small length of Wall have also been exposed to provide some insight into the rough and ready construction methods used by the Romans. Rough and ready their methods may have been but the Wall stood and it took a great deal of effort by those who used it as an unofficial quarry.

Next comes Heddon-on-the-Wall also freely accessible and maintained by English Heritage. Here, just to the east of the modern village and about half a mile to the south of the A69 is a well preserved section of Wall with a circular chamber close to the west end having served as a kiln during medieval times.

So far the Wall explorer has had free access — things change at Corbridge Roman town and museum where English Heritage require a fee. Here are good parking, toilets, a shop and some limited facilities for the disabled. The town was obviously not directly on the Wall but, as at South Shields, set back from the action. It was thus able to provide much more luxury as well as the essential back-up services. Between Good Friday or 1 April, whichever is earlier, to 30 September, Corbridge opens daily from 10 a.m. to 6 p.m. During the rest of the year it opens Tuesday to Sunday from 10 a.m. to 4 p.m. Corbridge was a vital link in the Roman supply line as it stood at the crossing of the Tyne and on the line of the Stanegate. From its origins as a fort it evolved into a large civil settlement. Among the excavated buildings is one of the best preserved granaries in Britain, and it is possible to see how the store was kept ventilated. Another treasure is the Corbridge Lion, a beautiful piece of sculpture originally designed as a fountain head. This shows that at Corbridge the architects had the time and peace to think artistically as well as to provide merely military protection.

Our next stop along the Wall is always at Brunton Turret, a lovely spot overlooked by trees and situated about half a mile to the south of Low Brunton on the A6079. There is parking on a layby, but this is very limited and you need to be fairly agile to reach the site which is freely open at all times. It is well worth a stop, however, as Brunton's Turret is one of the best preserved along the line of the Wall and there is also a 65-yard (60 metres) stretch of the Wall itself, giving a good chance to see the details of the construction.

One of the most impressive museums along the Wall is at Chesters, under the control of English Heritage, and for which a fee is required. It is situated at Chollerford about one mile west of the village on the B6318. Many visitors prefer to explore this section of the Wall by basing themselves at Hexham. We prefer, however, to drive along the whole length of the Wall which we feel gives the correct impression of the immense effort which was required to complete the enterprise. Cilurnum, as the Romans called it, was actually a substantial fort built astride the

The latrines at Housesteads fort on Hadrian's Wall.

Wall and it is open daily from Easter to September from 10 a.m. to 6 p.m. and in winter from 10 a.m. to 4 p.m. There is good parking, toilets and an excellent museum in which are many sculptures and inscriptions, and in summer refreshments are available. Outside the east gate of the fort is a good section of Wall plus a bath house which is one of the most complete Roman remains in Britain. Bathing to the Romans was not just a matter of cleanliness. It was their discussion room and was thus one of the most frequently used buildings of any fort. Other well preserved and excavated areas include the Commanding Officers' quarters which obviously had its own bath house, plus a system of barrack blocks. If Chesters was an example of a busy fort then a look at Black Carts Turret provides a contrast. Again English Heritage maintain the site and access is free at anytime, although parking can be a problem. It is situated $2\frac{1}{2}$ miles west of Chollerford on the B6318 and there is about a quarter of a mile stretch of Wall with the foundations of several turrets. What the soldiers thought of such a windswept period of duty after the luxury of the fort at Chesters we can but guess, but to the modern eye the views of the Wall overlooking green fields full of grazing sheep are a delight. We did visit the area once in winter with an icy wind blasting through the gaps in the masonry and it is this which probably made a more lasting impression on the troops. What they thought of the freezing waters of the River North Tyne is obviously not recorded; it looked beautiful to us with snow lying on its banks, but we had a warm car and a flask of hot coffee to look forward to.

At Carrowburgh, known to the Romans as Brocolitia, is a fine example of a temple dedicated to Mithras. It is also a demonstration of what can happen even when a site is in private hands. The owner allows free access and the site is maintained in such a way to ensure that it is being excavated slowly but properly. Where the original altars have been removed to the Museum of Antiquities in Newcastle copies have been placed on the site. Also in Newcastle is a scale model of the temple, yet another reason why we prefer to use Newcastle as our base for a systematic discovery of the Wall. Visitors are welcome to look around and no charge is made. Mithras was the Roman sun god and his temple looks beautiful when struck by an early morning light, as does what is left of a fort which once straddled the vallum. Brocolitia is reached along the B6318 about four miles to the west of Chollerford.

The next stop along the Wall is at Sewingshields milecastle just to the east of Housesteads and which was skilfully excavated in the late 1980s. It is freely open at anytime but there is no parking, although it is best seen by walking from Housesteads where there is a good Visitors' Centre and one of the best

Roman sites in Britain, and for which English Heritage charge an entry fee. It opens daily from 10 a.m. to 6 p.m. from Easter until September and 10 a.m. to 4 p.m. out of season. Once again the B6318 is the road to follow and Housesteads is almost three miles to the north east of Bardon Mill. It is the best known part of the Wall, probably because of its romantic position perched high on a ridge overlooking open moorland on which breed curlew and red grouse. The fort can also be used as a base for walks along the wall westwards to Steel Rigg and Sewingshields to the east. To the south of the site is a pay-and-display car park although the disabled can use a few spaces near the Visitors' Centre. The National Trust and the Northumberland National Park have provided a picnic site, shop, refreshment kiosk and Visitors' Centre, whilst English Heritage preserve the fabric of the fort. The remains are extensive and include the only example of a Roman hospital in Britain. The five acre site is shaped, as most large Roman forts were, like a playing card, within which are barrack blocks, commandant's house, granaries, gateways and street patterns. The site museum shows the original plan, a model of the fort and a wide collection of artefacts. The latter relate to both the military and civilian roles of Vercovicium which was the Roman name for Housesteads Fort.

For those who want to walk a stretch of the Wall then this is the place to do it and for part of the way you may well be in the company of much tougher treckers. The Pennine Way follows the Wall here for a few miles and this we describe briefly in our book *Discovering the Pennines*, a companion volume to the present work. This section of the Wall is owned by the National Trust and walkers are not charged a fee, although there are boxes into which donations may be placed. Housesteads is impressive and popular and the same is true of Vindolanda Fort and Museum also known as Chesterholme, which is sandwiched between the A69 and the B6318 around two miles north of Bardon Mill. Within the complex are the ruins of no fewer than eight forts and civilian settlements. Run by the Vindolanda Trust, the complex opens daily from 10 a.m. to 4 p.m. during February and November and gradually during the season the hours are increased. In July and August it remains open until 6.30 p.m. It is closed during December and January unless arrangements are made for pre-booked parties. Parking is by donation and the entry fee to the fort and museum includes a display showing full-scale replicas of the Wall in both stone and in turf which actually preceded it acting as a sort of template. There are examples of Roman writing tablets, textiles and wooden and leather artefacts. There is a picnic site, cafe, shop and good facilities for the disabled and for school visits. As with Cobridge, Vindolanda is not actually on the Wall, but the complex was originally set on Stanegate, and beside the road to the north east of the forts is a Roman milestone. As the Wall became important Vindolanda's function was changed and it acted as a storage and supply area plus a home for the troops and their families.

The stretch of Wall between Housesteads and Carvoran has much to offer, including some well preserved milecastles and turrets. At Cawfields there is a car park and picnic area maintained by Northumberland County Council to serve the visitors in search of the milecastle preserved by English Heritage. A small car parking fee is required but the site itself is always open and is free. A picnic site, toilets and Information board are provided and in the peak of the season a mobile Information Centre is also present. Cawfields, again reached along the B6318, is about 2 miles north of Haltwhistle. A little distance to the west is Great Chesters, the remains of a Roman Infantry fort named Aesica. This is on private farmland but the south gate is easily visible and the stretch of Wall at Walltown Crags, plus a turret, is freely accessible and is maintained by English Heritage. There is, however, limited parking, and the best place to conclude the discovery of the Northumbrian section of the Wall is by visiting the Roman Army Museum at Carvoran which is just beyond Walltown Crags which once more is positioned on the B6318. Thus it is possible to start a study of the Wall in the museum of Antiquities in Newcastle and finish in the museum at Carvoran. Here is a very large and lifelike reconstruction of a Roman barrack room, with a film theatre, and guided walks are available at certain times. The museum closes in January and February except by special appointment and then only between Monday and Friday. For the rest of the year it opens daily from 10 a.m. and closes at 5 p.m. except in the peak of the season when it opens until

Some areas of the Roman Wall and ditch are still present in windswept areas of moorland and need seeking out. This photograph shows an area close to Black Cart Turret near to Chollerford.

6 p.m. There is plenty of parking, good toilet facilities, disabled people are well looked after and there is a well stocked shop. Next to the museum is a fort which is at present awaiting the essential funds required to excavate it. We never mind paying to enter such places — the more money they get the more we shall all learn about one of the wonders of the world — Hadrian's Wall!

Apart from exploring this one long and almost continuous monument Newcastle can also be used as a base from which to explore a string of still attractive places which have stoutly resisted the spread of suburbia. Included are the castles at Aydon and Prudhoe, plus the villages where famous sons of the county were born. Two which should not be missed are Cherryburn near Mickley which gave us the artist in woodcuts, Thomas Bewick, and Wylam, the birthplace of George Stephenson, an artist in the use of heavy metal.

Aydon Castle is one of the most attractive and best preserved fortified manor houses in Britain, a tribute to the efforts of its early owners and since 1966 due to the staunch efforts of English Heritage. It opens daily from 10 a.m. to 6 p.m. from Easter to September and there is an entry fee. It is situated 1½ miles east of Corbridge and signed off both the A68 and B6321. It is set in a commanding position on the wooded slopes above the Cor Burn and was built at the end of the 13th century as a manor house rather than a castle by a wealthy merchant named Robert de Reymes. At this time it

This heron is a fine example of the work of Thomas Bewick.

was of timber but it was later strengthened in stone, though this did not stop it being ransacked and burned by the Scots in 1315. It was, however, repaired and probably strengthened, its original design probably being preserved, because it was used as a farmhouse during the 17th century, its owners not having the essential capital to carry out alterations. Thus many of its medieval features remain, including a magnificent Great Hall which is reached by an outside staircase. Provided on the site are refreshments, toilets, a shop, a living history education centre and good parking. Special parties are catered for even out of season.

Prudhoe castle in contrast is a 'true' castle and also looked after by English Heritage. It opens daily from April to September from 10 a.m. to 6 p.m., but from October to March it closes on Monday and its hours of opening are 10 a.m. to 4 p.m. Again refreshments are available; there is plenty of parking and a gift shop. Prudhoe stands on a wooded hillside dominating a crossing of the River Tyne. It proved to be so formidable that it twice successfully resisted attacks by King William of Scotland. The Gatehouse dates to the 12th-century and a 13th-century chapel was later built within the gatehouse.

Above the altar is an oriel window thought to be one of the oldest in England. Within the spacious inner courtyard is an 18th-century manor house — Georgian architecture at its best — and within this there is an exhibition which includes a video describing most of the Northumbrian castles. This is a treat not to be missed, especially in wet weather, whilst on more pleasant days the grounds are an ideal place to enjoy a leisurely picnic. The castle is situated on a minor road off the A695 and like many another in the county has intimate connections with the Percy family. They took possession in 1381, but fully realised its importance at times of border conflict, because it could control enemy movements in any direction be it north, south, east or west. Following the union of England and Scotland, Prudhoe fell on hard times although the Duke of Northumberland did build the manor house and also set in hand some restoration work to the old fabric between 1808 and 1820.

Few knew the wildlife of Northumberland better than Thomas Bewick (1753–1828) and his birthplace at Cherryburn is now administered by the Bewick Society. The house is situated on the south bank of the River Tyne twelve miles to the west of Newcastle. It is just off the A695 between Stocksfield and Prudhoe. It is well signed from Mickley Square and opens each day except Monday from 10 a.m. to 5 p.m. It does, however, open on Bank Holiday Mondays. The setting of Bewick's birthplace explains why he became interested in wildlife as it has beautiful views over the Tyne; since it opened in 1988 the reputation of Cherryburn has grown apace. There is an exhibition of his exquisite woodcuts, all of which can be viewed whilst listening to the muted background music played on small pipes. Using a drawing made by the artist's son the furnishings have been laid out as accurately as possible and there are fairly frequent demonstrations of the printing techniques used in Bewick's time. Outside there is a farmyard which is roughly cobbled and in residence are the usual variety of farm animals, many of which Thomas would have learned to draw as a child.

Thomas was the eldest of eight children in 1753 and went to the local school at Mickley where his talent for drawing was recognised. When paper was in short supply he drew on his school slate and he even admitted later in his life

WHITLAM
A Cheviot Ram belonging to M.ʳ Thoˢ Smith
of Woodhall
Taken in April 1792, when 7 Years old.

Thomas Bewick grew up close to Cheviot sheep and this engraving captures the ruff of wool around the neck which is typical of both rams and ewes.

that he was often scolded for drawing in chalk on the gravestones in Ovingham churchyard. Right from the start it was animals which fascinated him and which ultimately led to the illustrations in *The History of British Birds* which has remained a classic to the present time. We saved up long and hard to own a copy of this masterpiece which has pride of place on our shelves. Fortunately his parents gave his talents full reign and he was apprenticed to a coppersmith of Newcastle named Ralph Beilby. Although Thomas did not remain long with his master he was paid the then substantial sum of a guinea a week. After a brief spell in London Thomas returned to his beloved Northumberland and set up in business on his own account, in premises close to St Nicholas's church which has now been raised to the status of a Cathedral. The workshop has since been demolished, but the site is marked by a plaque. Each weekend Thomas walked home to Cherryburn to visit his family, a trip of around 20 miles, but the stroll must have provided him with much inspiration for his work, as Tyneside had not at that time become industrialised. He died in 1828 and is buried in Ovingham churchyard among the gravestones on which he had drawn as a child.

The church itself has a Saxon tower and inside there is now a memorial to Thomas Bewick. The Bewick collection is kept in the Newcastle Central Library, but the opening of Cherryburn as a museum has provided a much deserved memorial to a remarkable talent.

Another great, but quite different talent, was that of George Stephenson (1781–1848) who was also born not far from Prudhoe. In the village of Wylam the National Trust have preserved the cottage where he was born and there is also a railway museum here and another further down the Tyne at North Shields. George Stephenson did not have an easy start to life as his father was a low-paid miner and the lad was in every sense self-educated and could not read until he was 19. At the age of 12 George was herding cows on Throckley Fell for the sum of twopence per day. By the time of his death at the age of 67 his engineering skills had brought him a country estate at Tapton House near Chesterfield. In 1825 George reached the pinnacle of his career with the opening of the Stockton to Darlington railway with the inventor of the 'Rocket' himself driving the train of eleven wagons. George Stephenson's birthplace was a small red-roofed cottage standing by the river on what was once the main road through Wylam. The National Trust have restored one room of the cottage built around 1750 which is open from 1 p.m. to 5.30 p.m. between April and October on payment of a fee. Access to the cottage is on foot as it is on a walkway linking the riverside parks at Newburn and Low Prudhoe. At one time the wooden tramway ran from Wylam to Lemington and later William Hedley laid a rack rail and ran his 'Puffing Billy' along it. It was not only George Stephenson who had railways on his mind, and nobody interested in the history of railways can miss visiting Wylam and the little Railway Museum. It is situated on Falcon Terrace near the Fox and Hounds Inn. It opens all year on Tuesday and Thursday from 2 p.m. to 7.30 p.m. and on Saturdays from 9 a.m. to 12 noon. Entry is free but donations are welcome. The work of three railway pioneers are on display here —

Tynemouth Priory is a fine ruin and has changed little since this photograph was taken in the 1930's.

George Stephenson, T. Hackworth and William Hedley. For most of his life George Stephenson was associated with railways — all of his other feats of engineering stemmed from an idea to adapt the idea of locomotives on tracks from mines to a system able to carry passengers and goods around the country. It was this extension of the railways which allowed the Industrial Revolution to develop so quickly.

Whilst still a boy, George Stephenson started work at the same pit as his father and became so interested in the work as he drove his gin pony that he became known as a machine man of some genius and perhaps it was this which made him determined to strive for an education. By 1798 he was in charge of Hawthorn's pumping engines at Water Row Pit at Newburn, and by 1804 a further promotion had taken him to a job as a brakesman at Killington. Here his skill as a mechanic earned him the knickname of 'engine doctor'. George went on to build simple steam engines to haul coal from West Moor Colliery down to the River Tyne for shipment. The old horse-drawn wagons which his 'contrivances' replaced had a width of 4 feet 8½ inches and this is why all the large railways in the world today run on lines 4 feet 8½ inches wide! Visitors can stroll many of Stephenson's colliery wagonways which have now been converted into pleasant country walks. His home at this time was at Killingworth, being called Dial Cottage because of the sundial above the door. This dial was designed and made by George and his equally famous son Robert who was given an excellent education without ever losing his practical skills gained by contact with his father. Dial cottage is open to the public, and is linked by an old wagon walk to the Stephenson Railway Museum on Middle Engine Lane at North Shields. It was around these Northumbrian coalfields that railways were born. In 1815 William Hedley of Wylam built the 'Wylam Dily' which, although not very efficient, demonstrated that it was possible for iron wheels to get sufficient traction even on iron rails. This engine, continued in service at the Wylam colliery until 1862. The idea of cast iron rails and flanged wheels was found to work and this led Stephenson to build a locomotive called 'Blucher' for Sir Charles Liddell in 1814. Young Robert had been born in 1803 and must have been subjected to the hiss and clank of primitive locomotives from the day of his birth. By 1821 he was almost as famous as his father and went to South America in 1824 as a mining engineer, returning in 1827 two years after his father's triumph with the first passenger operated railway. By the 1830s George and Robert were a solid partnership, and as railways spread over the country like a spider's web they travelled widely and worked hard planning routes, overcoming engineering problems and building bridges as and when they arose and amassing a fortune. George Stephenson died in 1848 and was buried at Holy Trinity Church, Chesterfield, but when Robert died in the prime of his working life in 1859 he was buried in Westminster Abbey close beside Thomas Telford.

The Stephenson Railway Museum in Middle Engine Lane is a good place from which to begin an exploration of North Shields. The centre piece of the exhibition is *Killingworth Billy* built by Stephenson before 1826 and one of the world's oldest locomotives. Close by stands the massive *Silver Link* built more than a century later in 1938 and showing the

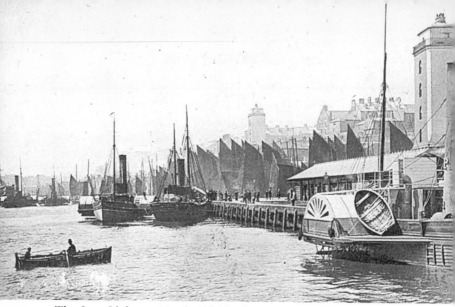

The Low Lights at North Shields close to the mouth of the Tyne in the early 1930's.

massive engineering strides which had been made. Here also on special weekends are ranks of well preserved traction engines and vintage cars. All that was lacking to complete this nostalgic visit was a ride on a steam train, but in 1991 this was put right by a link between Percy Main Station on the Metro system and the museum. Although most of the mines which inspired the railway dream have closed the site of High Pit at Killingworth is commemorated by a mounted colliery winding wheel.

North Shields is still a busy fishing port at the mouth of the Tyne close to Tynemouth. The Fish Quay is the place to be as the catches are landed, but only those who are prepared to get up early can enjoy this treat; for those on self-catering holidays or on their way home can re-stock their freezers at most attractive prices. The town's unofficial mascot is a statue called the 'Wooden Dolly'. She is a fishwife carrying a creel over her back. A creel is a large wickerwork basket used for carrying any heavy goods, including coal and fish. The original Dolly was designed by May Spence and was positioned at the end of a passage leading down to the quay, but Dolly became badly weathered. She was replaced by a statue which now stands in Northumberland Square. Still standing above the Fish Dock is the Wooden Dolly Pub. The seagoing tradition of North Shields is also exemplified by the High and Low Lights, two distinctive white towers built in the early 1800s. Ships' captains coming into the harbour kept the towers in line and knew that they were in the deep water channel and clear of the dangerous rocks just below the surface of the shallow estuary. Large ships also use the harbours, especially the ferries to Scandinavia. We have often travelled to Norway both for pleasure and on business and we always use the trips to explore North Shields, and also Tynemouth, which has much to offer the tourist. The best way to appreciate the history of Tyneside is to take a cruise up river from either South or North Shields on the Tyne and Wear Ferries which run a regular Sunday trip during the summer. The trip takes about four hours, the vessels are comfortable and details can be obtained by ringing the Tyne and Wear Transport Executive on 091 2610431.

Tynemouth castle and priory still dominate a magnificent headland overlooking this pleasant town as they have done for centuries. Many kings of ancient Northumbria are buried among the ruins of the castle and priory looking out over the estuary of the Tyne. There have been fortifications here for more than 1,300 years and each time the fierce Danes wrought destruction the Northumbrians raised them from the ashes. Even as recently as the First World War the site was strengthend to provide protection for vessels using the Tyne and some of the reconstructed magazines can still be seen. The Benedictine priory was built around 1090 as a replacement for the Saxon monastery which had been abandoned in 1008. Both the priory and the adjacent castle show medieval building at its best. The huge castle gatehouse still stands, and much still remains of the priory including the presbytery, attached to which is a 15th-century chapel. Robert de Mowbray founded the priory which was dissolved on the orders of Henry VIII in 1539. Both this and the castle are now preserved by English Heritage and are open daily from April to September from 10 a.m. to 6 p.m. Out of season the opening hours are from Tuesday to Sunday from 10 a.m. to 4 p.m. It is worth the small entry fee just for the view over the magnificent beaches of Long Sands and King Edwards Bay which are becoming increasingly popular with holidaymakers, especially those who like windsurfing and yachting. There is an open-air swimming pool at the end of the

Long Sands. For those who want to explore historical sites then Tynemouth has more to offer than most resorts.

The Collingwood monument is a tribute to the Northumbrian Admiral Lord Collingwood born in 1748 who led the British Fleet into the battle of Trafalgar in 1805. His flagship was the *Royal Sovereign* and canons from this vessel have been incorporated into the statue which looks out over the river and is close to the Watch House which is the headquarters of the Tynemouth volunteer Life Brigade, the first such body in Britain which is still active today. Inside are relics from ships which were wrecked on the infamous Black Midden Rocks which can be seen from a point below the Watch House.

As we have seen, Tyneside played its part in the development of passenger railways, and its still operational station is a museum piece in its own right. It was opened by the North Eastern Railway Company in 1882 and was largely responsible for opening up Tynemouth as a holiday resort for the hardworking people of Tyneside. The station, with its cast-iron elegance and glass roof, has been restored to all its old glory and is said to be the finest remaining example of a Victorian station. On Saturdays there is often a flea market and it is used to house special events throughout the year. These are well advertised locally.

A serious rival to Tynemouth as a seaside resort is Whitley Bay, but we feel that the two should be considered as one complete complex rather than rivals because they are so different. There is a direct link to Newcastle via the Metro system, the station being close to the beach; There is also good parking. There are plenty of guest houses and hotels and in summer every spare space seems to be full of flowers. The sands are excellent and the sea safe for bathing. Whatever the weather Whitley Bay has the answer with Spanish City, Leisure Pool, Holiday Centre, an ice rink and the Playhouse Theatre. At Spanish City is a Grade II listed pavilion around which has been built all the fun of the fair with side shows and amusements cheek-by-jowl with fast food outlets, but the area retains an air of good taste. At the Leisure Pool is a sloping beach where toddlers can splash about in safety; there is also a wave machine and swirling water slide. There are sunbeds, saunas, Turkish baths and several cafes and bars where the lost moisture can be replaced. The Holiday Centre is a luxurious caravan park with its own in-house entertainments, although the Centre is also popular with non-residents. Behind the Spanish City is the Playhouse Theatre which is used by both amateur and professional groups and there are also film shows on offer. The Whitley Bay Warriors have their home rink here which is open for all skaters whatever their proficiency or otherwise. Our favourite walk from Whitley Bay is out to St Mary's Island and Lighthouse reached by causeway only at low tide and which was once used by smugglers to land their contraband. The lighthouse was built in 1898 in an attempt to prevent ships hitting the dangerous rocks which fringe the island. The lighthouse is no longer used but is open to the public, and it is worth the effort to climb the steps to the lantern room from which there are magnificent views both to seaward and landward. The keepers' houses have been converted into a Visitors' Centre in which there are exhibitions of history and natural history. There is a stone house on the island which was once an Inn but has unfortunately lost its licence. Between Whitley Bay and Tynemouth is the fishing village of Cullercoats which has a magnificent sandy bay. The harbour was also used for the export of salt and coal, but all that remains today are the remnants of the fishing industry and tourism. This is a feature of modern Northumberland — its ability to adapt, improvise and above all to conserve memories of its illustrious past.

CHAPTER 4

Kielder Water and the North Tyne

The normal way to discover a new area, or indeed to plan a guide book is to make several visits, read many books and allow your feelings to develop. Kielder Water does not allow this method to be followed since it was only opened by the Queen in 1982 as a water supply for the thirsty industries around Newcastle. Alas these have fallen victim to the depression and new uses for the largest man-made stretch of inland water in Europe have had to be searched for. There was only one answer — tourism — and developments are likely to continue well into the 20th century. Whilst preparing this book we wrote to the Tourist Board and this resulted in a letter from Anthony Murray inviting us to tour Kielder Water aboard the vessel *Osprey*, which began operating tourist trips from June 1991, and of which he is master. We chose a glorious summer's day in late June when Northumberland seemed to be the only place in England not to be sheltering from a deluge! This we have found often to be the case and no one should be afraid to holiday in this area because of the weather. Later in the summer we returned to Kielder to make a television film and enjoyed a delightful barbecue on an evening cruise on the ferry *Osprey*.

Looking at the area from Tower Knowle close to the *Osprey's* berth, Kielder reminded us of a Swiss lake with the blue waters reflecting colourful boats of all shapes and sizes. It was almost impossible to remember what the area was once like — here were quarries and coal mines with the last drift mine only closing in 1990 and a network of industrial railway lines which closed in 1956. Some of these scars were hidden by 120 million conifers which were planted from 1926 as a result of the activities of the Forestry Commission. This body has been savaged by naturalists, many of whom know nothing of the Commission's original brief. At the end of the First World War the supplies of timber in Britain were exhausted and new trees had to be planted. Everyone knew that native broadleaved trees were the answer, but they take more than a century to mature.

This is why fast-growing alien conifers such as Japanese larch and sitka spruce were planted along with one of Britain's three native species, the Scots pine. All three are now being harvested and the timber used to produce pulp for paper. The initial idea was to produce timber and not to think of the aesthetic factor. In retrospect we find it hard to disagree with the initial concept, nor with the aggressive policy of keeping walkers away from the saplings. This led to bad feeling between the Commission and the general public and we sometimes feel that the official body has done more to heal these early wounds than has the naturalist . What has been done cannot be undone. As the first crops are being harvested much more consideration is being given to which species are planted where. Nowhere is this more obvious than in the vast Kielder forest, with the new tourist trap around the reservoir generating much more co-operation. Around the lake it is still possible to see the original planting plan. Japanese larch was set around the edge of the forest to act as a windbreak. Larch is also planted in blocks between the sitka spruce as its timber does not burn so easily. Sitka spruce is by far the fastest growing conifer and can be cropped at around 50 years, whilst the native Scots pine was planted in smaller numbers probably as a compromise to divert some of the opposition.

The history of the maturing forest and the new reservoir is best appreciated starting at the Visitors' Centre at Tower Knowle from which the 27 miles of shore line can be examined on a map which also features on the free leaflet. There is a good audiovisual presentation, a souvenir shop and an excellent cafe and restaurant. There is an Information Centre which is an ideal starting point for those wishing to stay in an area which has now realised that it is beautiful and no longer scarred by industry, and bed and breakfast accommodation of high quality is evolving to serve a need. Kielder water can be explored by car as there are many secluded picnic parks, on foot or by the ferry. By far the best way is by a combination of foot and ferry since the round trip by the *Osprey* allows the journey to be broken and rejoined at any point. Many walk between one ferry point and the next. A recently developed addition is Kielder Bikes Cycle Hire service situated close to the reservoir dam. The recommended route is flat and so ideal for those who are

Work in progress night and day to construct the valve tower at Kielder
Water. (Photograph by permission of Northumbrian Water)

afraid of hills and traffic. The service operates throughout most of the year, but those interested should book their bike by ringing 0434 220392.

Before we set out for the 1¼-hour tour of the reservoir on the *Osprey* Anthony Murray told us to keep an eye open for Leaplish Waterside Park, Hawkhirst Adventure Camp, Matthew Linn, the North Shore Complex and Kielder Castle. After this the *Osprey* swings across the water to Plashetts, Benny Shank Belling before returning to Tower Knowle via the dam and valve tower. Anthony also told us that the *Osprey* was built by Marshall Branson Marine at Amble and that she was named after the bird of prey which is recorded fishing in Kielder Water almost every spring. So far as aquatic life is concerned the water is too clear, too acidic, and too deep to be attractive to birds but in time nutrients will build up and the bird counts will be bound to rise. Northumbrian Water are beginning to look for outlets for their surplus water and have even exported some to Gibraltar. Some idea of the capacity of Kielder is realised by the fact that if every human being in the world flushed a toilet at the same time, the demand could be met!

Leaplish Waterside Park answers all the needs of the young at heart and those seeking entertainment for an active family. If it is water sports you need, be it by boat, canoe, sailboard, or bobbing about in a wet suit, then here is your chance. There is a cafe, a bar and a shop plus a variety of comfortable log cabins available for hire, plus a camp and caravan site. The whole complex has a distinctly Scandinavian feel about it, as has the nearby Scout Adventure camp at Hawkhirst which opened in 1982. Obviously Scout groups use the centre but its residential facilities based upon the Sunley Centre can be hired by other youth groups of up to 40 people who can self-cater or be looked after. Here are a wide selection of sailing dinghies and canoes, camping is available at reasonable rates, and visitors are welcome on payment of a small fee. Beyond Hawkhirst is Matthew Linn which has a large car park and picnic area, thus providing a base for anglers and walkers. Permits for fishing are available on site, and boats can also be hired. The best walk leads to Lewisburn where we once watched crossbills feeding on a crisp January morning, whilst in the following May the same tree contained the nest of a sparrowhawk. Beyond the bridge

Looking like the ribs of a whale, this picture shows work in progress on the Kielder Dam Culvert in June 1977. (Photograph by permission of Northumbrian Water)

at Lewisburn is Bakethin reservoir which is a shallow extension of Kielder and has been set aside as a nature reserve to which access has sensibly been restricted. There are, however, plenty of splendid views from the track of the now disused North Tyne railway and especially from the Kielder viaduct.

The traffic-free northern shoreline of Kielder Water is overlooked by Kielder Castle, the Forestry Commission's Visitors' Centre which has plenty of secluded car parking. Within the castle are displays of wildlife and detailed explanations of ancient and modern forestry techniques, plus lecture and audiovisual rooms and a cafe which, like that at Tower Knowle, is cleaner, cheaper and better than those in many other parts of Britain. Kielder's is not a typical Northumbrian castle of ancient lineage but a Gothic style shooting box constructed for the use of the Duke of Northumberland in 1775. For those wanting to spend time seriously observing wildlife it is possible to hire a seat in one of a number of well sited observation hides. Although traffic is largely restricted a toll road leads from the castle through the forest a distance of almost 12 miles to Redesdale where it joins the A68 close to another reservoir at Catcleugh. The roads hereabouts are usually quiet, with a notable exception being during the RAC rally when protesting machinery screams and echoes along the forest roads of the Kielder Forest. Byreness church built in the 18th century is worth a visit because of a stained glass window which dominates the little building and depicts the workers and the tools they used to construct Catcleugh reservoir between 1890 and 1905. During the main period of construction 500 men were employed and they had with them their wives and children. The project involved damming the River Rede and there was one camp of workers on either side. The two sides were great rivals and were known as 'Newcastle' and 'Gateshead'. The labour was hard, the living conditions were far from good, and resulted in at least 60 deaths. Those who perished are remembered in the stained glass of Byrness and also by a brass plaque. The church is kept locked but the key is available from a garage and snack bar close by on the A68. At one time the church was the smallest in the diocese of Newcastle and it was first built as a chapel of Ease to the ancient parish of Elsdon. The churchyard at Byrness, however, is of ancient origin, perhaps even Saxon. Our last visit to the charming little church was on a hot August bank holiday when we still found quiet solitude in and around the picnic site at Raw next to the church.

Although building the reservoir was dangerous in itself there was more threat from the living conditions and many men and their dependants fell victim to disease. Many who died of cholera are buried in an unmarked grave close to St Oswald's church in Bellingham.

This is a good point to discuss the latest reservoir scheme at Kielder which was first suggested in 1853 by a schoolmaster to the North Shields Water Company who were urged to dam the North Tyne valley close to the village of Kielder. The village is situated not far from the castle. The project began in February 1975. The dam commenced in April 1976 and the reservoir was filled during the spring of 1982. At the peak of the work

The Ferry Osprey prepares to depart on an evening barbecue cruise around a peaceful Kielder Water on a gentle August evening.

some 750 men and women were employed many travelling by road and rail each day from southern Scotland and northern England. Communications were good enough to avoid the problems of the late 19th century and of course the equipment was much more powerful. What did all this effort and energy produce? Statistics they say prove anything but there is no arguing with a dam 1250 yards long, 170 feet high and 423 yards wide (1142.5 × 51.8 × 386.6 metres) constructed of 5.3 million cubic yards (4.05 million cu/metres) of whinstone, river sand, clay and gravel. It holds back 44,000 million gallons of water, occupying 2,684 acres (1086 hectares) and some 7½ miles in length. The tower, which contains pumps to extract water is 226 feet (69 metres) tall and releases a controlled quantity back into the North Tyne. The river is then used as a source for the rivers Wear and Tees, the water being extracted via a pumping station at Riding Mill, whilst water for Tyneside is extracted from the area of the North Tyne between Wylam and Ovingham. Despite these demands there is still plenty of surplus water.

This is not surprising when the expanse of the lake is viewed from the ferry which serves tea, sandwiches and a variety of alcoholic drinks, and also provides an informative taped commentary. The crew are interested, knowledgeable and always ready to talk Kielder folklore. We can all ignore the fable of the Kielder rabbit first spotted by the miners and quarrymen and which is said to be over five feet long! (nearly 2 metres). This says more for the local beer than it does for the natural history. The scars of industry become apparent as the ferry approaches Plashett's quarry from which $7\frac{1}{2}$ million tons of whinsill rock was extracted for the dam. Black streaks in the rock indicate the presence of coal but the village now lies below the surface of the reservoir. Some 14 families were evacuated during the construction and their ancestors had worked in brickworks as well as in mining, the products being exported via a rail link which only closed in 1956. The old track is now in use as a forest road, close to which is a picnic site from which there is such a pleasant lakeside walk making it well worthwhile to break the ferry tour for an hour or so. The wildlife is surprisingly rich here and there are foxes, badgers and roe deer but alas no Kielder rabbits! There are also walks from the jetties at Benny Shank and Belling. Belling takes its name from the Bell miners who dug coal from below the ground which eventually collapsed to produce a bell-shaped depression. The Belling inlet is one of the most sheltered areas of Kielder and Belling Crag was popular with rock climbers prior to flooding. The combination of industrial archaeology, modern technology and natural history ensures an increasing stream of school visits. Visitors staying in the area should keep their eye on the noticeboard in Northumbria Water's Visitors' Centre for details of evening cruises and barbecues. No area in the whole of Britain is developing more quickly than Kielder and new schemes are developing all the time. High Yarrow Farm close to Tower Knowle specialises in visits for children and reindeer are occasionally summered here along with less exotic species. Forest drives are available in a horse and trap, one of the best ways we know of exploring the Kielder area — a mode of transport almost totally ignored by animals and birds. The increasing popularity of Kielder is having a beneficial effect on small local settlements such as Elsdon, Otterburn, Simonburn, Bellingham, Wark-on-Tyne and Chollerford, whilst Hexham, which rightly claims to be the capital of Tynedale, must also welcome the increasing popularity of the man-made lake.

Otterburn is yet another Northumbrian village which was the focus of a fierce battle, the probable site being about one mile west of the village and

> This deed was done at Otterbourne
> About the breaking of the day
> Earl Douglas was buried at the bracken bush
> And the Percy had captive away.

The battle was fought on 19 August 1388 and the Scots inflicted a heavy defeat on the English. The victors did, however, lose one of their bravest leaders, the Earl of Douglas. The spot at which the brave man fell is marked by Percy's cross (what a pity it is not Douglas's cross) which is set in woodland close to the A696, and for which a car park, picnic tables and an information board have been provided. The conflict, which was fought in full moonlight, has become known as the Chevy Chase, and the ballad written to commemorate the titanic struggle between Harry Hotspur and James the Earl of Douglas is now the traditional tune of the Northumbrian Pipers.

It is surprising that the Scots won because immediately prior to the fight they had marched 30 miles across tough border country. The Scots were ambushed; Douglas, as a premonition had told him, was run through by a Percy sword. Then without a leader the Scots rallied and put the English to flight, leaving the river running red with blood. This is the stuff of legend and Sir Walter Scott made full use of available fact and his own poetic licence. Two villages associated with the battle are Elsdon, where many of the dead were buried, and Otterburn, from which the battle takes its name:

> Have ye ivver been to Elsdon?
> The world's unfinish'd neuk;
> It stands among the hungry hills
> An' wears a frozen leuk.

This charming verse is only true in winter. Elsdon built around its 7½-acre green was the medieval capital of Redesdale.

Kielder Castle, now the headquarters of the Forestry Commission was once a shooting lodge.

The verse is quoted on a leaflet on sale in the parish church of St Cuthbert. There is evidence of a church here since St Cuthbert's body was rested on its way to from Lindisfarne, pursued by the Danes. The present church, in the form of a simple cross, was built around 1400 as a replacement for a Norman church which was probably destroyed by the Scots. The pele tower, built to protect the vicar, was probably

Elsdon church overlooking one of the finest village greens in England.

constructed at the same time as the church. It is one of the best examples of such a building to be found in the county and is still a private residence. St Cuthbert's stands in a magnificent position and has a 17th century bellcote topped by a small spire and decorated with stone balls. Much of the original architecture remains, but there was an essential restoration in 1810 during which more than 100 skeletons were found buried close to the north wall. Forensic evidence shows that they were those of young men and are probably of those who perished during the battle of Otterburn which is described later in this chapter. The church also has the skulls of three horses found in the belfry in 1827 and said to have been brought here either to keep away lightning or to improve the acoustics of the church. How either of these aims could have been achieved is beyond us. Behind the church are two mounds known as the Mote Hills — all that remains of a once formidable Norman motte and Bailey castle from which the area was ruled and which was probably built around 1080. The dominant family hereabouts was the Umfravilles whose crest can be seen on the walls of the vicar's pele tower. It is likely that the Saxons had a settlement here and the dominance of the castle did not last long. It was dismantled around 1157 when a huge castle was built at Harbottle. The name Elsdon probably derives from the Saxon 'Dene of Ellers', meaning a wooded valley dominated by alders, although other historians suggest it is also Anglo-Saxon, but from 'elde' and 'dun' meaning a fort on a hill. Either of these seem possible but we can discount the resident giant by the name Ella who legend suggests terrorised the district.

At one time Elsdon had an important market and was also on an ancient drove road, which may account for the solid circular stone cattle pound into which stray beasts could be driven through a narrow entrance. Just outside the village is a grizzly reminder of a violent past on the road signed to Cambo. Winter's Gibbet and Stang Cross is maintained by the National Trust. In 1791 the body of William Winter was hung here in chains after he had been found guilty of the murder of Margaret Crozier of Elsdon at this very spot. The present gibbet was erected on the site of the original, and from it hangs a rather bizarre looking model head which certainly adds a feeling of foreboding to this windswept hill. There is a large block of stone at the foot of the gibbet and this is thought to be the base of a Saxon cross which marked the highest point on the drove road. Along this road the cattle bred in Scotland were driven to the lucrative English markets once peace was the rule rather than the exception. About a mile further on towards Cambo a group of four trees is all that remains of the smithy where the cattle were shod to prepare them for the long journey, and shoes have been found on the site.

The village of Otterburn, set almost at the junction of the Otterburn with the River Rede, is a pleasantly airy little spot with a long old main street, behind which are modern houses. Two buildings are of interest — the ancient Otterburn Tower Hotel and the more modern Otterburn Mill. There has been a dwelling on the site of the tower since 1076, but the present building was constructed around a 14th-century pele recently restored to produce a delightful hotel standing in its own attractive gardens. The Tower was damaged by the Scots at the time of the battle, but its walls proved stout enough to prevent

Elsdon church across the village green photographed from inside the medieval cattle pound.

a total breach. Among its later owners were the Hall family and 'Mad Jack Hall' left Otterburn to join the 1715 rebellion. He was hanged at Tyburn for his part in the tragic event. For many years visitors have ignored the tower, which also serves excellent teas, and searched out Otterburn Mill, long famous for its tweeds, and delightfully situated near the bridge. The reputation of the Waddel family's tweeds was based upon the wool sheared from the local black-faced sheep. Alas the mill no longer weaves on its own account, but imports material for the shop from Scotland. However, the quality of the tweed is such that a constant stream of visitors is ensured.

The leaflet on sale in St Mungo's church describes the nearby great Parish of Simonburn from Hadrian's Wall to Carter Bar and is more of a comment on the past than the present. These days Simonburn is too often ignored by tourists, and there are few more delightful scenes than the village green overlooked by low whitewashed cottages, many of which have colourful gardens. St Mungo's, best viewed through the lych gate, was built in the 13th century, but substantial repair work and some rebuilding took place in 1762 and 1863. There was obviously a church on the site in Saxon times and this is proved by carved stones dating back to the 8th and 9th centuries and set into a niche in the porch.

Scholars have suggested the main cross to be the work of the Tyne school begun by Italian masons brought to Hexham by St Wilfrid around AD 690 and attracted the interest of Acca who was bishop at Hexham from AD 709 to 732. By this time the Angles had established the Kingdom of Northumbria and had been converted to Christianity.

The interior is interesting for two main reasons. The floor actually slopes from west to east as St Mungo's was actually built on an incline. There is a fine example of a double piscina set into the sanctuary wall. There is a neat little car park just beyond the church and walks from here lead up to crags on which stand the Goat Stones — four standing blocks and the remnants of a stone circle. There is also the small stark ruin of Simonburn castle reached along a much easier walk. It was said to hold such a vast treasure that the whole of Northumberland could be purchased with it. No wonder the last attack upon it was not by the Scots but by avaricious villagers.

Bellingham is yet another settlement claiming to be the 'capital' of part of Northumberland; this time of North Tynedale, and leaving Hexham to its claim to rule the whole of Tynedale both north and south. We have known Bellingham for many years but only learned to appreciate it whilst writing *The Pennines*, a companion volume to the present book. We learned its folklore

Elsdon pele, one of the finest such buildings in Northumberland and still in use as a residence.

and its just as fascinating history plus the even more exciting discovery of the countryside around it. The present book gave us another excuse to polish our walking boots and use Bellingham as a base from which to explore Riding Wood, Ealingham Rigg, Hareshaw Linn and the River North Tyne, all of which are the subject of informative leaflets produced by the Bellingham and District Tourism and Trade Association, and can be purchased from the Information Centre and local shops. We had two days in March and two more in July during which time we did each walk twice. We even learned to pronounce the name properly — locals say Bellin-jum.

The return trip to Riding Wood is around four miles but there are plenty of excuses to stop *en route* — discoverers like us do not have to be hikers. Although not open to the public Hesleyside Hall can be seen and the ancestral home of the Charlton family contains an historic relic with a tale to tell. It was a custom in this lawless border country for the lady to serve a spur on a covered tureen to let the men know it was time for them to restock the larder. This was often done by raiding the farms over the Scottish border and returning laden with beef and mutton. The Scots were not averse to their own spot of armed rustling and this led to the development of bastles as opposed to castles. A bastle was not even as substantial as a pele tower but was a fortified farmhouse of two storeys, the farmer living above and his livestock quartered below. Riding Farm, situated close to the route to the wood, incorporates part of an old bastle. Riding is a typical north-country wood consisting of rather stunted sessile oak plus silver birch many of which are parasitised by bracket fungus. This is sometimes called dryad's saddle or razor-strop fungus. A dryad was a fairy and the fungus was actually used when dried and hardened to sharpen cut-throat razors and knives. Many of the oak show the results of attacks by galls, which are tiny wasps which lay their eggs within the delicate tissues of the leaves. The oak responds by growing protective tissue around the egg on which the developing larva feeds. This cancerous growth stops once the young wasp hatches and eats its way out of the gall. Scientists are obviously interested to know what chemical the oak produces to stop the growth.

Inside the wood is the site of a rectangular Romano-British settlement within which are the remains of four round stone houses. After crossing the old disused track of the Border Counties Railway the return route to Bellingham passes under the North Tyne Bridge built in 1843 and then follows the edge of the Jubilee Field which was only laid out in 1977 to celebrate Queen Elizabeth's Silver Jubilee. In Bellingham, close to modern garages, is an ancient well known since the middle ages as Cuddy's well. Its waters, thought to have healing powers, are still used for baptisms in St Cuthbert's church.

Winter's Gibbet stands close to the base of a Saxon cross on the moorland road between Elsdon and Cambo.

Ealingham Rigg is best strolled in fine weather and in winter the upland track affords excellent views of Bellingham. A height of 789 feet (240.3 metres) is reached and part of the walk follows the Pennine Way. There is plenty of heather here which is at its best in late summer and which is burnt every seven years or so to produce food for red grouse which thrive on the succulent young shoots. There are plenty of damp areas on the uplands and these create breeding grounds for frogs; aeshna dragonflies are also a feature here. Birdwatchers have good hunting here and species regularly recorded include kestrel, wheatear, lapwing, skylark, meadow pipit and barn owls are increasing in numbers since they became almost extinct in the 1960s. Rabbits are common here, as are brown hare and short-tailed field vole, whilst their predators include fox, weasel and stoat. There are good views of the North Tyne river on its way down from Kielder. The path also runs close to the Forestry Commission offices and workshops which opened in 1986.

Northumberland is not noted for its waterfalls but Hareshaw Linn in times of flood can indeed be dramatic. It is reached along a track of just over a mile from Bellingham, which follows the Hareshaw Burn, a tributary of the North Tyne. Alongside the stream is Hareshaw Dene, an attractive area of woodland now designated as a Site of Special Scientific Interest (SSSI) owned by the county council and administered by the National Park Authority. Its beauty is very obvious but close observation reveals that the area was once heavily industrialised. A row of old stone cottages were once the offices of Hareshaw Ironworks which opened in 1840, and it was here that the iron was forged to build Newcastle's High Level bridge. Near to the cottages are the remains of the coke ovens which produced the fuel for the three blast furnaces. The coal from which the coke was made came from Plashetts Colliery now, as we have seen on the banks of Kielder Water. Prior to the discovery of the method of producing coke, charcoal was used, and this caused great damage to Britain's woodland. Smelting iron required plenty of air which was pumped into the furnace by bellows driven by a waterwheel, and traces of this can be discovered. The ironworks at Hareshaw did not thrive for very long and closed in 1848, since which time the area has recovered its haunting wildness

Otterburn tower, now a hotel, is another example of an ancient Pele tower put to good use.

examplified by Hareshaw Linn — linn being an old English name for a waterfall. Although only about 30 feet (10 metres) high, Hareshaw is impressive and well worth the walk; even though it is a cul-de-sac route the walk is interesting enough to reveal new treasures on the way back to Bellingham. The main river of the town is the North Tyne, and yet another attractive walk follows this and the route passes its confluence with the Hareshaw Burn. The walk of around three miles also follows part of the old track of the Border Counties Railway, opened in 1862, which ran from Hexham to Ridcarton Junction in Scotland, passing through the North Tyne valley. The impetus for the construction of the railway was to link the woollen mills of the Tweed valley with the fuel supplies around Kielder, especially Plashetts Colliery. The mines proved, however, to produce household coal and not the type suitable for boilers. The link survived until 1958 but with no passengers carried after 1956. Bellingham's station is now used as a maintenance depot used by the County Council's Highways' Department. What a pity that part of the line could not be revived as a steam route linked to the new tourist attraction at Kielder.

An exploration of the town itself should begin at the old market place which is dominated by a memorial to those who fell in the Boer War, close to which is the village (or should it be the town?) hall with its wooden cupola and clock. Between the war memorial and the road is a most unusual weapon mounted in a wooden frame. It is a gingall, — a mounted musket from China captured during the troubles of 1900. It was presented to Bellingham by Commander E. Charlton of HMS *Orlando*. Down from the square is the quaint little church of St Cuthbert, cramped between the narrow road, old cottages and new houses. The church is unique in having a heavy stone-flagged roof — a useful defence against the fire-raising Scots, and which has been kept in a good state of repair. Because of the weight the whole building was buttressed in the 18th century and skilful repair work was carried out in more recent times. It is in the churchyard, however, that one of Bellingham's most fascinating features is to be found, known as the 'Long' or the 'Lang Pack'. The tale of this unusual gravestone tells of an 18th-century pedlar who called at the home of Colonel Ridley at Lee Hall. The colonel had made a considerable fortune in India and the pedlar, pretending to be in need of a night's lodgings, had his greedy eyes on the colonel's possessions. The colonel was not at home but his maid Alice allowed the pedlar to enter and to lay his long pack on the floor of the kitchen. Later she saw the pack twitch and called the ploughboy who blasted it with his gun; a groan came from the pack and it began to ooze blood. Realising that a raid on the property was imminent, the servants set a trap and drove off the burglars. The accomplice in the pack, whose job was to have opened the door, died and was buried in the churchyard and topped with a stone shaped like a long pack. Reached by a winding path from the church is St Cuthbert's well mentioned earlier in this chapter and which in medieval times was thought to have healing powers; we can vouch for the fact that it tastes as if it contains some interesting minerals. The reason why Bellingham became an important settlement was because of its bridge over the North Tyne, the first recorded span being a wooden structure of the 12th

Just outside Otterburn stands Percy's cross, surrounded by trees and marking the site on which Douglas of Scotland was killed.

century, although Saxons used the ford from the 6th century. The present stone bridge dates to 1835.

Wark, now a quiet village in North Tynedale, was the scene of the murder of the Christian King Alfwald of Northumbria in AD 788 and thus allowing the area to slide backwards into paganism. An unintentional link with un-Christian activities is found today in the delightful Tonehaugh picnic site. This is on the banks of the Wark Burn, another tributary of the North Tyne, and features an attractive collection of decorative Totem poles. This area attracts naturalists, many of whom have read the works of Abel Chapman whose *Bird Life of the Borders* was published in 1889. Abel is buried in Wark churchard. Born at nearby Houxty, Chapman achieved world-wide fame as a writer and collector of specimens from all over the world. Many of his specimens are on display at the Hancock Museum in Newcastle and are known as *Abel's Ark*. The Normans had a castle at Wark but little remains today except a grassy mound overlooking the river. A narrow iron bridge gives a unique feel to the village, made up of a huddle of cottages. On the eastern bank of the river, about one mile from Wark, is Chipchase Castle, a mansion dovetailed in 1621 to a 14th-century pele tower. Chipchase can easily be seen from the road.

A visit to Haining Farm Park is to be recommended for families. It opens daily between Easter and 30 September between 1.30 p.m. and 5 p.m. On display are deer and rare breeds of sheep and pigs.

Chollerford has a long and distinguished military history beginning with the battle of Heavenfield in AD 634. Just outside the village on the B6318 a plain wooden cross marks the site of the battle at which King Oswald defeated the heathen King Cadwallon and made Northumbria safe for Christians.

The political situation at his period was critical and the Christian Kingdom of Northumberland then spread from Edinburgh to the Humber. It was well governed by Edwin who had descended from the Angles who had filled the vacuum left by the Romans and had embraced the Christian faith. This led to a confrontation with the pagan Celts who wished to keep to the old religion and had no intention of allowing either the Angles or Christianity to flourish. Both Cadwallon of Gyynedd, which is now in Wales, and Penda of Mercia, now known as the

Midlands, were so worried by the expansion of Northumbrian influence that they attacked the forces of King Edwin and his son, both of whom were killed near Doncaster in AD 633. This heavy and demoralising defeat led to a period of slaughter and destruction by Cadwallon, and this split Northumbria into its two original Kingdoms of Bernicia and Deira. Nobody was able to resist this fragmentation, and both of Edwin's direct heirs — his cousin Osric and his nephew Earfrid — were killed. The remaining link with the good old Christian days was the 29-year-old Prince Oswald, who had been educated by the monks on Iona off the coastline of Mull. Oswald answered the call of his heritage and set up a base at Bamburgh before marching south to rendezvous with his supporters in the North Tyne Valley. Cadwallon, no mean leader himself, had anticipated Oswald's deployment and marched from York along Dere Street, the old Roman road, and challenged the Christians at Hefanfelk which we now know as Heavenfield. At this time it seems that the Roman wall was still fully intact and Oswald used it to protect his flank and force the Celts to move in a predictable direction. Oswald erected a simple cross where the church which bears his sacred name now stands and both he and his troops prayed for victory. Obviously aware that there could be no further chance of saving Northumbria the Christians charged and the Celts were routed. They were pursued over a wide area and large numbers of skulls, bones, sword hilts and other weaponry have been unearthed over the intervening centuries. Cadwallon's men made a desperate last stand at Hallingdon, some five miles to the north, but the pagan king himself was killed on the banks of the Rowley Burn about three miles to the south of Hexham.

The result of this battle was so conclusive that Oswald was able to ask St Aidan to journey from Iona and set up a monastery on Lindisfarne which went on to prove itself to be a Holy Island from which Christianity spread dramatically. Oswald deserved to be made a saint and Heavenfield should be regarded as one of the most significant battles ever fought on British soil.

The B6318 is on the line of the military road built to the plan of General Wade following the Jacobite rebellion of 1745 when troop movements were restricted by poor roads. The road crosses the River North Tyne at Chollerford, which had a military tradition from Roman times when the river bank was the site of a magnificent fort known then as Cilurnum and now as Chesters. Chesters became a country house with the remnants of the fort preserved in the grounds, but one of the former owners, John Clayton, was an enthusiastic and able archaeologist who was born in 1792. Without his work Chesters would not be the important Roman site that it is today. It is a Mecca for students of the Roman Wall which was described in detail in Chapter 3. Clayton collected many artefacts but also restored the bath house and on the opposite bank the remnants of the Roman bridge abutment. Now run by English Heritage, Cilurnum at its peak housed 500 troops, occupied $5\frac{3}{4}$ acres, guarded the river crossing and was the largest fort in Northumberland. Chesters, the home of John Clayton, who died in 1890, is a classical 18th-century mansion, but our favourite site at Chollerford is the Roman bridge reached by crossing the modern road bridge near the George Inn and then following the footpath along the disused railway from which there are splendid views across the river to Chesters. All the villages described in this chapter, and also Kielder Water, are best explored from a base at the attractive market town of Hexham itself, the site of a famous battle.

Hexham is regarded as a turning point in the Wars of the Roses, not because of it being a mighty battle, but because it led eventually to the death of the Lancastrian King, Henry VI. The site of the battle, Hexham Levels, is easy to find, being situated about two miles south-east of the town on the B6306 road to Slaley. Here Linnel's Bridge crosses Devil's Water, another attractive tributary of the North Tyne. About a quarter of a mile along a cart track leads to the Levels, above which to the left is Dipton Wood from which the Yorkists charged and inflicted heavy losses on the Lancastrians who were trapped in a ravine with a steep bank at their backs. The Lancastrians had also just completed a series of long marches and were outnumbered. King Henry VI was no leader and his general, the Duke of Somerset, had everything stacked against him. He was captured after the battle, in which he was wounded, and taken back to Hexham, where he was summarily tried and executed. Henry VI escaped and headed towards the

Simonburn is one of the finest little churches in Northumberland.
There has been a religious house here since Saxon times.

Lancashire-Yorkshire border where he had friends. He was sheltered at Bolton-by-Bowland near Clitheroe, but he also had enemies whose efforts resulted in his capture whilst crossing stepping stones over the River Ribble at nearby Brungerley. He was taken back to London where he was killed, and thus the battle of Hexham was a tragedy for the Lancastrian cause.

Hexham is a town set on a hillside, having its market day on Tuesday with early closing on Thursday. It is an important cattle and sheep market and is the focus for south-western Northumberland as it has been since the 7th century when its splendid abbey was established. It originated around AD 675 at the instigation of St Wilfrid and within it there are many interesting Roman stones suggesting an even earlier settlement. Most historians, however, are of the opinion that the stones were probably brought from Corbridge. It is probable that Wilfrid's church was built from stones removed from the Roman fort. The early design was obviously influenced by Roman buildings and was described by Eddius who praised Wilfrid for building a house 'in honour of St Andrew the Apostle. My feeble tongue will not permit me to enlarge here upon the depths of the foundations in the earth, and its crypts of wonderfully dressed stones, and in the manifold buildings above the ground, supported by various columns and many side aisles . . . Nor have we heard of any house on this side of the Alps built on such a scale.' Alas, in 875 Halfdene the Dane swept through Northumbria, Hexham church was burned, and although some attempts were made to re-establish its old glory these were not really successful and it was not until the Augustinians were given the land that the present building was begun. What did survive the Danish attack, however, was the crypt, and this is the finest such Saxon structure to be found in Britain. Other reminders of the Saxon period are an eastern apse, a solid looking font, a frith otherwise known as 'peace stool' and a rare example of a chalice. There is also Acca's cross set up in AD 740 to mark the grave of Wilfrid's successor. Thomas, Archbishop of York gave Hexham to the Augustinians in 1113 and they set about producing a Priory of great architectual merit, much of their work remaining to delight the modern-day pilgrim seeking a period of quiet from the busy market place overlooked by the abbey. The choir

The Anglian cross in the porch of the church at Simonburn.

is particularly beautiful and dates back to the 13th century, although the roof is some 200 years later. leading down into the choir are the monks' night stairs from the dormitory and it is said that they are haunted. Whether this is true or not is open to debate, but they are certainly well worn. The stairs are the most photographed features of the abbey, along with a huge Roman tombstone, although the church authorities do not encourage photography. This may help boost the sales of guidebooks and postcards in the excellent little cathedral shop. The set of 38 medieval carved seats called misericords are remarkable, as are screens and painted panels, which makes it difficult to understand why many benches were ripped out and sold for firewood during the 1868 restoration. There is also some fine stonework at Hexham, including Prior Rowland Leschman's 15th-century chantry which contains some caricatures of St Christopher, St George and the mythical dragon, plus some genuine animals, including a fox preaching to a flock of geese, no doubt with evil thoughts running through its mind. The human trends of gluttony, vanity, piety and purity are also humourously depicted. When Henry VIII dissolved the abbeys in the 1530s Hexham's church survived, as it was used as the local parish church. It is not only the abbey which used local Roman settlements as an unofficial quarry.

The best starting point for a tour of Hexham is the market-place bordered by a covered shambles, the Abbey itself and the Moot Hall built in the 14th century. It is now a gallery in which a variety of changing exhibitions are held during the year and, as we shall see later, the home of a fascinating library. An attractive archway in the hall leads to the Manor office, once the jail and now the compact Tourist Information Centre and also the Border History Museum. It opens between Easter and October from Monday to Saturday, plus Sundays on holiday weekends. The hours of opening are from 10 a.m. to 4.30 p.m. Between February and Easter and in November it opens on Monday and Tuesdays between 10 a.m. and 4.30 p.m. and party visits should be pre-booked. The building was constructed in 1330 from stones taken from the Roman camps; it was the first gaol in England to be purpose-built, and it served its original function until 1824. Since it opened in 1980 the Border History Museum has been laid out on three floors. It

The Chinese gun at Bellingham is one of the most unusual weapons to be seen anywhere in Britain.

has been skilfully designed and describes the turbulent period of Anglo-Scottish history which ebbed and flowed across the border county. Here are weapons and the armour, ancient skulls and modern audiovisual presentations. The conditions in the old gaol can be seen by looking down through a grating in the floor. Audiovisual presentations explain the life of the border reivers — the word meaning a cattle thief. Membership does not seem to have been restricted to one class, and peers of the realm and agricultural labourers all seem to have made a good living by taking advantage of a fluctuating border with nobody around to apply the law of either Kingdom. Some farmers were prepared to pay a ransom of black cattle — or mails — to be left alone. Here we have the origin of the word blackmail. Many farmhouses were strengthened and a window from these battle houses is on display in the museum. Hexham has lived in peace since 1761 when rioting miners shed so much blood that the Riot Act

One of the finest Roman tombstones to be found in Britain is the large block found in the south transept of Hexham Priory.

was read in the market place. The men from Allendale were
objecting to recruitment into the local militia and 300 people
were injured and over 50 killed. Ever after the North Yorkshire
militia were known as the Hexham Butchers. Hexham really is
the place to discover the history of the area because the Border
Library is housed in the 14th-century Moot hall, which is open
Wednesday and Thursday between 11 a.m. and 3.30 p.m. It is
a reference collection only, but staff are available and always
willing to answer queries. It was originally the private collection
of William V. Butler, former director of the Northumbria
Tourist Board. Apart from books and manuscripts on the
area there are also sections on poetry, folklore, dialect, sheet
music, records and taped material with the Northumberland
Pipes featuring very strongly. There is also a fine collection
of archive photographs, slides, newspaper cuttings and maps.
Anyone wishing to discover the border region from southern
Scotland to north Yorkshire cannot afford to miss this library
or the Border History Museum.

In addition to its ancient buildings put to such good use
Hexham has some fine 19th-century buildings which prove that
not all Victorian architecture was poor — a 19th-century wool
warehouse has been converted into a 20th-century up-market
swimming pool which won a design award in 1975. The abbey
grounds are overlooked by a modern bandstand, and the Town
Hall, built in 1866, was designed to look like a French chateau,
usually known as the Queen's Hall. It is now an arts' centre with
a library and a well-appointed theatre. There is a restaurant and
the centre is open daily from 9 a.m. to 11 p.m.

Around Hexham there is a perfect combination of history
and natural history, and in the Chollerford area there are the
Hexham Herb Garden and Nursery for which there is a small
entry fee including access to a wild woodland walk. It opens
from 10 a.m. to 5 p.m. daily, from March to October, but
with shorter opening hours in winter. The garden won a gold
award at the Gateshead Garden Centre in 1990. The two-acre
walled garden contains a good collection of herbs, plus a rather
spectacular rose garden. Because it is so close to the Roman fort
at Chesters the garden has produced a display of plants which
the Romans cultivated in Britain. There is also an Elizabethan
Knot Garden. The old English word for a bunch of flowers

was a knot, and hence the rhyme 'Here we go gathering knots in May' now makes sense. The garden specialises in varieties of the delightfully scented thyme family and the National Thyme Collection is situated here. The woodland walk is dominated by beech, not a common tree in Northumberland, and on one winter visit we watched a flock of bramblings feeding on the triangular beech nuts which are also attractive to their near relatives, the much commoner chaffinch.

CHAPTER 5

Around Morpeth

Always an important market town, Morpeth had greatness thrust upon it when the boundary changes of 1974 pushed Newcastle into Tyne and Wear and Morpeth became the undisputed county town of Northumberland. In this book we refuse to move Newcastle, but we have no wish to insult this attractive town which lies on a sweeping bend of the River Wansbeck. Market day is Wednesday and early closing is Thursday. In the 16th century Leland, one of the greatest travellers of his age, wrote

> Morpet, a market town is XII long miles from New Castle. Wansbeke, a praty ryver, rynnith threge the syde of the towne. On the hyther syde of the ryver is the principall churche of the towne. On the same syde is the fayre castle standing upon a hill, longing with the towns to the Lord Dacres of Gilsland. The towne is longe and metely well builded with lowe housus, the streets pavyed. It is a far fayrer town than Alnwicke.

Actually there should be no rivalry between the two — Alnwick is a delight and set among idyllic scenery, whilst Morpeth is a miracle, having survived in all or most of its glory despite the expanding industry which still dominates much of the south of the county. Morpeth has some fine buildings, including the clock tower, town hall, chantry, the privately owned castle and the parish church of St Mary. The clock tower was built of stone taken from the Oldgate Gatehouse in 1604. The lower portion was used as a gaol and the town stocks were situated outside the door. In 1705 a top storey was added to make room for a set of bells which were recast in 1951 and continue to ring a curfew each night at 8 p.m. The clock tower overlooks the market square and the town hall also has a prominent position here. It was built in 1714 having been designed by Vanburgh, but was renewed following a fire in 1869/70, the plans being drawn up by a less imaginative architect named Johnson. There is an open stone-flagged hall leading off the main street which was once the butter market, and on the first floor is a fine ballroom, the original Vanburgh council chamber and the Mayoral chamber in which the town's impressive insignia and plate are displayed. Our best memory of Morpeth was on a glorious morning in early May when the whole town seemed smothered in flowers and it was easy to understand why it won the Britain in Bloom Best Small Town trophy in 1989. As usual, during our journeys of discovery, we began at the Tourist Information Centre which at Morpeth is something special, being situated in a very historic building, the Chantry of All Saints and the nearby bridge associated with it, but of which only the cut waters remain. The chantry was probably in existence by 1300 and the list of recorded Chaplains begins in 1310. The Chantry was dissolved in 1552 and its funds and building were used to found the free Grammar School although of the original building only the north wall and the porch to the west remain intact, although much of the stone was re-used. One of the school's most famous pupils was William Turner, often regarded as the father of English botany — thus Northumberland nurtured a theoretical botanist and in Capability Brown the foremost landscape gardener of his age. William Turner (1510–68) was a belligerent Protestant and during the time that Mary Tudor was trying to re-establish Catholicism many scholars fled to Europe. It was whilst studying in Bologna with Luca Ghini that Turner gained his knowledge and love of plants which he put to such good use on his return to England. The Chantry now serves as a combination of Tourist Information Centre and museum. Of particular and unique interest is the bagpipe museum which tells the story of 'the wailing bag' including of course the Northumberland small-pipes. Those who complain about the sound of bagpipes of all shapes and sizes should take the trouble to listen to the music and set it into the context of the wild and wonderful countryside. In this environment pipe music is indeed soul-stirring.

The Northumbrian Craft-Centre offers a varied collection of local crafts with many items for sale, and thus this area is popular with local people, but especially with tourists. On the day of our last visit we were enthralled by horn walking sticks, hand painted china, patchwork, pictures and prints, pottery, stained glass, ceramics, wood turning, leatherwork, toys, photographs of stunning quality and wonderful examples of calligraphy. Only the best are allowed to exhibit here, and the contributors are being added to all the time. William Turner would be pleased to see the exhibitions of pressed and dried flowers. Other famous inhabitants of Morpeth from later centuries include Admiral Collingwood, who took over command when Nelson was killed at Trafalgar in 1805. Lord Cuthbert Collingwood was born in Newcastle in 1748. Milburn House now stands on the site of his birth but on the outside is a bust to commemorate the event. Also a native of Morpeth was the suffragette who killed herself by diving in front of King George V's horse running in the Derby of 1913. Emily Davison is buried in the churchyard of St Mary's church, her resting place still kept as a tidy memorial to her convictions. St Mary's church is built on a hill to the west of the town and it is mainly a 14th-century building, but there are many traces of an earlier structure. One tradition of St Mary's is that when a newly married couple emerge from the church they find that local children have tied the gates with rope and this is only slackened when the appropriate fee has been paid. This reminds us of Chipping in Lancashire where the tradition is known as 'perrying'. A more chilling aspect found in the churchyard is a watch tower dated 1831 and built to keep a lookout for body snatchers. A good price was paid by surgeons for a body which could be dissected for the benefit of their students. Although St Mary's has been extensively restored it does have some reminders of its 14th-century origins, including an octagonal font and the Jesse Window, said by many to be the finest example of medieval glass to be found in the whole of Northumberland. The church is now difficult to find in the sense that it is surrounded by a large modern housing estate, and the nearby Morpeth Castle alas is not open to the public, although Carlisle Park which it overlooks is attractive at any time, but especially in summer when it is a riot of colour. A castle existed at Morpeth as early as the late 11th century but little remains of the original building or indeed of the 14th-century fortification. The 14th-century gatehouse was restored to produce a fine house in 1857 and is still lived in. It can, however, be seen from the footpath to the west of the castle and there are also good views of the River Wansbeck. Nearer to the town centre traffic is carried over the river by Telford's attractive bridge built in 1831, the replacement for the original Chantry bridge now only serving pedestrians. In truth it was never designed to serve any other function.

Carlisle Park was officially opened in 1929 and was laid out on land given to the town in 1916 by the Earl of Carlisle. It functions as a recreational lung for the local people and visitors alike and includes tennis courts, bowling greens, a paddling pool and extensive and colourful gardens. A walk from the park leads to Newminster Bridge and to what is left of Newminster Abbey, a Cistercian house established in 1138. The abbey suffered frequently at the hands of the Scots and consequently never became rich; it was dissolved in 1538. Henry VIII's men reduced it to rubble but excavations recently have shown a ground plan of a once substantial building. What an architectural heritage was destroyed during Henry's attack on the abbeys.

Another important building in the town itself is found on Castle Square and was formerly the Court House designed by John Dobson in 1821; until 1881 it was the town gaol. After the prisoners were transferred to Newcastle the building was the magistrates' court but the Grade II listed structure has now been converted to produce luxury flats, function room and a restaurant with a fine reputation.

The Morpeth area is dominated by two main rivers, the Wansbeck and the Blythe, the latter being the more industrialised of the two.

From Fernirigg the Wansbeck flows through the Whelpingtons, South Middleton and Low Angerton where it is joined by the Hartburn. Having absorbed this tributary it flows on to Mitford where it is joined by the River Font. From Morpeth the Wansbeck reaches the sea via Ashington and Newbiggin-by-the-sea which should both be included within the broad definition of 'Wansbeckdale'. Although Kirkwhelpington was once a mining village it has in recent years reverted to its former rural charm and is still dominated by the Norman church of St Bartholomew. The low broad tower is heavily buttressed and this and the long nave only having a central aisle are both signs of medieval strength; there are two medieval bells which still

Cambo is a village of pretty cottages and colourful gardens, a fitting memorial to Capability Brown.

bear the original inscriptions. Sir Charles Parsons, one of those involved in the development of the turbine engine, is buried here, as is the Rev. John Hodgson who was vicar here during the period 1823–34. During this time he wrote his classic work *The History of Northumberland*. He was, in fact, a local lad, born at nearby Hartburn. This lovely village stands proud on a hilltop close to the confluence of the Hartburn with the Wansbeck. Close to the river is an 18th-century tower built by the Vicar, Dr Sharpe. The church dates to the 13th century, is dedicated to St Andrew, and contains a memorial to John Hodgson, its most famous son. Actually the church was consecrated early in the 11th century and two skeletons found in the tower are of this period. The Normans ousted the Saxons, and in 1207 King John gave the living to Tynemouth Priory. In 1255 the living changed hands again when Henry III gave Hartburn to St Albans' abbey, the tithes to be used to provide their visitors with a supply of 'bread and ale'. This is a church full of interesting furniture, including Florentine lamps, Napoleonic banners and with the stones also having a tale to tell with a number of carvings, particularly of fish used as a Christian symbol and several very obvious masons' marks.

Another village near Kirkwhelpington has provided an even more famous son: Lancelot 'Capability Brown' was born in 1715 at Kirkharle. No doubt the pretty countryside around his native hamlet and the village of Cambo where he went to school influenced his appreciation of plants, as must also have been the case with William Turner. Lancelot left school at 16 and was given the post of apprentice gardener to Sir William Loraine who had a relatively small estate at Kirkharle. The school is now the village hall and the upland settlement of 18th-century terraced cottages is in the care of the National Trust. The beauty of the gardens around the cottages and below the church at Cambo are a delight and would please its most famous son if he could be brought back for the summer months. It is a comforting thought that 'Capability's' memory is preserved for ever, but the post office is also worth a close look as it is based around a medieval pele tower. The young Brown spent six years at Kirkharle and he must have been given much encouragement, his work still clearly evident from an elevated viewpoint close to St Wilfred's church. His fame spread rapidly and he was appointed to the estate of William Kent at Stowe and was ever after in such demand by rich southerners that he never returned to Northumberland on a permanent basis. He did some work for Sir Robert Shafto at Benwell Tower on the north bank of the Tyne but not much remains of his work. From 1765, however, he worked on the estate of Sir Walter Blackett based on Wallington Hall, and around the same period he planned the gardens of Alnwick Castle. Both these works are permanent memorials to his craft, but apart from a sandstone block close to the B6342 there is no memorial to one of Northumberland's most famous sons. It is difficult to see how a museum could have been set up to a man whose work was so obviously out of doors. We feel that Wallington Hall is the best memorial within the county. Now owned by the National Trust, Wallington Hall is open daily between 17 April and 30 September, except Tuesdays, and for the rest of the year it opens on Wednesday, Saturday and Sunday. The grounds, walled garden and conservatory are open daily and are famous for their fuscias and of course as an exhibition of the skills of Capability. Wallington and Cambo together provide one of the most beautiful areas in Northumberland, the estate belonging in the 14th century to Alan Strother whose name was used by Chaucer to describe one of his rogues in *The Reeves Tale*. No doubt there was a building here at this time but the present mansion dates from 1688 although it was substantially altered to a design by William Paine in the mid 18th century. At one time Wallington belonged to Sir John Fenwick who was beheaded for rebelling against King William III and Queen Mary. At the end of the 18th century, his estate was purchased by Sir William Blackett who had made a substantial fortune from coal mining and shipping. Sir Walter Blackett died childless in 1777 and the estate passed to his nephew, Sir John Trevelyan. From then until 1936, when Sir Charles Trevelyan gave the estate to the national Trust, the family, which included G. M. Trevelyan the famous historian, remained in occupation. It is thus fitting that the building contains a series of murals in the central hall by the Newcastle artist, William Bell Scott, which tell the long history of Northumberland. Included are the building of Hadrian's Wall and the death of the Venerable Bede. There are also on display some exceptionally beautiful plasterwork and a famous collection of porcelain. The dolls' house collection is also famous, as is the display of coaches, which is both comprehensive and colourful. The shop and cafe are both popular, especially at the time of the Wallington Festival or when open-air performances of Shakespeare are held on the spacious lawns. This is strolling country, whilst for those who prefer to stretch their limbs Rothley Crags is a perfect spot, and was once an integral part of the estate. The climb provides panoramic views and leads to a prehistoric hill fort hanging over the precipitous western face. In medieval times there was

THE OLD
CAMBO SCHOOLHOUSE
ALTERED & ENLARGED TO A
HALL & READING ROOM
BY SIR GEORGE OTTO TREVELYAN BART
1911

LANCELOT BROWN
KNOWN AS CAPABILITY BROWN
THE LANDSCAPE GARDENER
BORN AT KIRKHARLE IN 1716
ATTENDED SCHOOL
HERE

A memorial to a capable gardener on the wall of his old school at Cambo.

a deer park here, whilst on the summit was a beacon to provide warning of the approach of the Scottish army. Rothley lake, designed by Capability Brown, is a good place for a spot of winter birdwatching or for a springtime flower hunt, and also nearby are a couple of Castle Follies. Codger's Fort, now owned by the National Trust, was built in 1769, and Rothley castle, now almost crumbling away, was designed by Daniel Garrett around 1740. Both do, however, look more 'authentic' than they actually are.

A more historic ruin is found at Mitford which once commanded the confluence of the River Font with the Wansbeck, but in the 14th century it was literally devastated by the Scots and was not restored; little remains today, but its original strategic importance can easily be appreciated.

Beyond Morpeth the Wansbeck flows on through Ashington to Newbiggin-by-the-Sea. Mention Ashington to people who do not know much about Northumberland and they will first refer to Jack and Bobby Charlton who came from this cradle of football and then perhaps to the dramatically political miners' galas which are held in the town. This is true mining country with serried rows of terraced housing and pitheads arranged on the banks of the Wansbeck. If you want to see miners at play then watch the young play football and visit the allotments and talk to the gardeners who nearly all specialise in growing the most enormous leeks. These days the mining industry has declined, although there is also more pride in conservation and alongside the river are good walks and recreational facilities. Close by is the village of Woodhorn which has a Saxon church and a Colliery Museum. Woodhorn means a 'wooded point of land' and the Saxon church has been dated to the 8th century and is said by historians to be the oldest on the Northumbrian coast, which is certainly remarkable in an area noted for its religious houses.

St Mary's was declared redundant in 1973, since when it has functioned as a museum, cultural centre and private chapel, although it is used for services during the traditional festivals. There is free parking and admission, and there is a sales point for books and for locally made crafts which make excellent presents or reminders of a day spent discovering the history of the area long before industry paid its disruptive visit. The museum has been laid out without destroying the fabric or the atmosphere of the building's architecture which is an attractive blend of Saxon, Norman and Gothic styles. There is also a fine recumbent effigy of Agnes de Valence, the wife of Hugh Balliol, who was the brother of the King of Scotland. There is a medieval bell inscribed 'Ava Maria', thought to be one of the earliest to be found in the county. St Mary's is open all the year from Wednesday to Sunday plus Bank Holidays from 10 a.m. to 12.30 p.m. and from 1 p.m. to 4 p.m.

In direct contrast, Woodhorn also has the Colliery Museum situated within a recently developed Country Park, and which is freely open from 10 a.m. to 4 p.m. all the year round, from Wednesday to Sunday plus Bank Holidays. We think this is one of the best exhibitions to be found in Northumberland. It describes the industrial and social history of the area, using life-sized models and audiovisual displays, but even more importantly there are plenty of contemporary artefacts on display. Atmosphere is created by the presence of a working forge near the old stables for the pit ponies, with the smith now producing a variety of items for sale. A woodworker also provides items made in a traditional joiner's shop also once a vital part of any mining complex. The Ashington artists were living proof that although all miners had to be tough, many were highly intelligent people who had fruitful leisure activities once their hard underground labour was finished for the day. Between 1934 and 1984 the Ashington artists produced a remarkable visual record of life in and around a pit village and examples of their work are on display.

Great strides have recently been made to improve the environment between Ashington and Newbiggin-by-the-Sea and the two-mile stretch of the Wansbeck bank has been transformed. This riverside park is becoming ever more pretty, partly because of mine closures and partly due to imaginative effort and enthusiasm on the part of the local people and their elected representatives. To the north of Ashington a huge spoil heap has been landscaped to form a country park and a 40-acre lake has been developed in a subsidence dip and is used both for sailing and windsurfing. This is also a refuge for seabirds and wildfowl, especially when they need shelter from the gales battering the coast of the North Sea. Newbiggin simply means a 'new building' and originated in the 12th century as an offshoot to the south of Woodhorn. By 1203 it was sufficiently important to be granted a fair and market charter. St Bartholomew's church, which stands on a headland, has for centuries been an important landmark for shipping. The origins of the

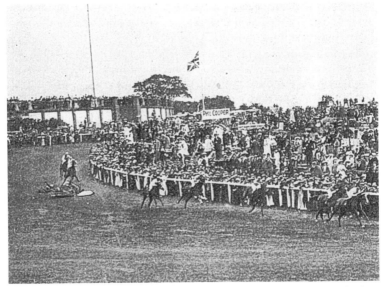

Miss Emily Davison threw herself under the King's horse during the 1913 Derby. This historic photograph shows the incident as the horse, well down the field, rounded Tattenham corner. Both horse and jockeys were injured and Emily died four days later.

religious site, however, go back well beyond the early 13th century and there was a Saxon settlement here called South Wallerick. The Danes sacked the village in AD 875 and some say the replacement settlement was called the 'Newbeginning' and several alterations in spelling have occurred since. This may be a fanciful derivation but isn't it attractive? The original Saxon church was a chapel-of-ease built by the monks of Lindisfarne. In the Middle Ages Newbiggin was a vitally important port for exporting grain and it also had a period when it was dominated by coal. There is still an aluminium smelting works to the south of Newbiggin-by-the-Sea, but this marks the end of the present industrial belt. Here, as we shall see later, the River Blythe has been very much a working river, but to the north of Newbiggin there begins one of the most attractive stretches of coastline to be found anywhere in Britain, and which is described in later chapters. Newbiggin has made several attempts to establish itself as a seaside resort but its recent efforts have brought much more success.

Although much of the effect of the industry which blighted the Blythe valley can still be detected, great ecological improvements have been made recently. It has to be admitted, however, that the closure of many mines has caused a rise in unemployment and ripped the heart out of many village communities. Although the area around any mine is an ugly scar on the landscape there were attractive and unspoiled areas of countryside between, which the miners were quick to appreciate. One can hardly be surprised at this, considering the men spent many hours deep in the bowels of the earth, and fresh air must have been like an essential drug.

In the upper reaches of the Blythe valley near Belsay is Bolam Lake Country Park, some 37 hectares (92.5 acres) of artificial lake created in 1818 by John Dobson. Part of the lake has been set aside as a sanctuary which many birds take advantage of in winter and several species such as moorhen, coot, great crested grebe, little grebe and mallard breed. The water is fringed by reeds and surrounded by woodland. It is open all year and there is a substantial car park, close to which is the warden's office which provides much useful information. Close by is Belsay Hall, Castle and Gardens administered by English Heritage. The complex is open daily between April and September and on Sunday afternoons between October and March. The castle is a 14th-century border town house and the floors and roof have been renewed, but unfortunately little now remains of the attached and once substantial manor house added in 1614. In front of the main block there was a formal garden and at the rear is a Victorian model farm which is a real piece of social history. There are substantial earthworks in the park which show that the area was settled long before the Middleton family established their hold over the area. Belsay Hall, some distance from the castle complex, is one of the most important neo-classical houses in Britain being built between 1810 and 1817. This interesting architectual style has been continued in the adjacent village which has an arcaded terrace. The architect of the house was actually a relative of the Middleton family, Sir Charles Monk, but he freely acknowledged his debt to the more famous John Dobson. The

Whalton's midsummer Baal fire ceremony photographed in the early 1900's.

skill of the builder can easily be seen at Belsay because the house is not furnished. Not all the grounds are open, but 30 acres give more than a flavour of past glory; the quarry garden shelters many exotic species and there are colourful displays of roses, rhododendrons, meadow flowers and a winter garden. Meldon Park, which has been the home of the Cookson family since 1832, is another example of the work of John Dobson who, in Georgian times, had a fine reputation in the North East of England. The house is situated between the Rivers Blyth and Wansbeck and is open the last week in May, the first three weeks in June plus the August Bank Holiday weekend. It opens from Saturday to Monday between 2 p.m. and 5 p.m. The gardens are open from the last week in May until September, from 2 p.m. to 5 p.m. Monday to Friday only.

Meldon, only 7 miles west of Morpeth on the B6343, is worth the planning needed to make sure it is open and also the entry fee, for here is a 'lived in' late Georgian mansion of great charm. The staircase is rightly famous, as is the magnificent hall, which is a good example of the work of Lutyens, dating to the early years of the 20th century. It is not only the house which is attractive; there are also gardens and woodland walks, all of which are open to disabled visitors who are particularly well looked after at Meldon Park. We just wish it was open more often and for longer periods. The wild garden and the kitchen garden are particularly attractive and a good place for budding botanists and horticulturalists to learn their craft.

The work of Sir Edwin Lutyens is also on permanent exhibition in the estate village of Whalton with its delightfully spacious main street dominated by the manor house created by combining a group of existing cottages at the end. This work was completed in 1908. The garden was designed by Gertrude Jekyll whose reputation in her age rivalled Capability Brown in his, although she usually worked on a much smaller scale.

The 4 July is widely known as an American day of celebration but at Whalton a ceremony is held dating back at least to Saxon times but probably long before — indeed nobody seems to know the origin of the Baal fire. There seems little doubt that the huge bonfire lit as the sun goes down has its origins way back in pagan times and was originally part of the Midsummer's Eve celebrations. Before the modern calendar came into operation the 4 July was, in fact, Midsummer's Day.

A few years ago nobody in their right mind would have wished to discover the lower reaches of the Blythe, but what a change has come about in the late 1980s and early 1990s. The area now has much to offer the traveller and the tourist, especially those interested in industrial archaeology, but also those who love wild life, whilst those who enjoy quiet sandy beaches are not disappointed either. The two large settlements are Bedlington and Blythe itself which is an ideal base to explore southwards along the coast and inland to Cramlington.

Almost as large as Ashington, Bedlington was the focus for a huge mining complex, and it is here in June that the miners' picnic, perhaps better known as a gala, provides a focus for political speeches. Banners fly in the breeze and brass bands play together, the fierce competition of the concerts forgotten for a day of glorious sound. Children and adults dress in their Sunday best and the dogs, including whippets and the local breed of Bedlington terrier, are held on a tight leash. The wide main street is perfect for such a gathering which developed during the 19th century. The history of the town is much older than this, although until coal became King Bedlington was

Blythe harbour literally at full steam in the 1930's.

little more than a village. St Cutherbert's was dedicated around AD 900 and there are still some traces of its Saxon origins as well as some interesting Norman work. At one time the area was part of the County Palatine of Durham at which time it would have been in the midst of a wild area known as Bedlingtonshire and it was at this time that the Bedlington terrier was developed to play its part in the hunt. Much unspoiled countryside still remains and there is a good walking area based upon the Country Park at Hornford Mill off Church Lane. Here there is a good information centre, nature trails, picnic area and facilities for horse riding. On the western outskirts is Plessey Woods Country Park which has a small camp site and Visitors' Centre from which several footpaths lead out into the woods. Plessey Mill can also be seen on the banks of the River Blyth and in the 41 hectares (102 acres) both red squirrel and roe deer are found, together with breeding tawny owl, sparrowhawk, grey wagtail and dipper.

Blyth itself has much to offer and now has a large beach only slightly sprinkled with coal dust and stretching some two miles northwards to the Wansbeck estuary. On the beach, rocks shelter the north harbour with the modern town built mainly in the 19th century seen across the water. The distance by small ferry is only about 100 yards (32 metres) but it is some five miles by road. The main harbour area is still busy exporting some coal and importing timber and alumina but in the south harbour nestle scores of pleasure craft and here are the headquarters of the Northumberland Yacht Club based in a now redundant light ship. A small harbour existed here in medieval times and Blyth is said to mean 'white water', perhaps because of the water crashing on the rocks or equally possibly on account of the crashing waters of the upper reaches of the river. There was some export of salt in, and probably before, 1208. To evaporate sea water to produce salt required fuel and once wood supplies were threatened it was easy to hack away at the out-croppings of coal. There was also a small fishing fleet and for a time there was an important shipbuilding yard which constructed the second *Ark Royal*. The town is at last showing pride in its past and the Blyth Town Museum on Croft Street covers the history of the area, concentrating on 19th- and early 20th-century developments. The John Sinclair Railway museum on Princess Louise Road concentrates on memorabilia of the North Eastern Railway in general and the Blyth and Tyne branch in particular. It is claimed that an inclined rail was operating at Blyth in the early 17th century to run coal down to the harbour, it being relatively easy to push the empty wagons back up the track. Like any harbour facing the North Sea Blyth had to be given protection during the war and the substantial gun emplacements and look-outs can still be seen on the links fringing the town. Yet another glorious beach runs south to Seaton Sluice and in the hot days of high summer and with blue sky and white-capped waves the scene is reminiscent of Australia with muscular life-guards patrolling the area.

Seaton, like Blyth, is also making an excellent job of repairing the scars of its industrial past. Huge blocks of dressed stone have protected the harbour since 1660 when Sir Ralph Delaval built a harbour from which to export coal and salt, but silting up of the channel always seems to have been a problem. It was decided to construct a sluice gate and a narrow canal to provide a second route to the sea. Silting won, however. The canal is now itself full of silt and the sluice which added its name to that of Seaton has long gone. On the harbour there is a tourist information point and it is good to see that some atmosphere and colour have been maintained despite the loss of the shipbuilding yard, the salt export industry and the village bottle factory. There is good walking from Seaton Sluice including Earnshaw Walk, a one-mile circular starting at the entrance to Holywell Dean. The name Earnshaw is of interest as 'Earn' was the name for the sea eagle now extinct in England and Shaw means 'a word'. Eaglewood, however, still has much to excite the naturalist. Charley's Garden has also gone, but the walk to the column of sandstone rock in Collywell Bay is also invigorating. Charlie Dockwray once cultivated a small garden in this potentially difficult spot. The one place in the area which cannot be missed is Seaton Deleval Hall, the home of Lord Hastings, and regarded by many as the masterpiece of Sir John Vanbrugh whose other famous houses included Blenheim Place and Castle Howard. Seaton Deleval was built between 1718 and 1728 and both the Hall and its impressive gardens are open in the summer, but not on a regular basis. Times can be found from the information centres in the area, but discoverers need not be disappointed if it closed because there is plenty to see around the area. Vanbrugh actually died before the house was finished and fires in 1752 and 1822 did sufficient damage to reduce the magnificence of Seaton Delaval. The west wing is still an imposing residence and many of the furnishings and fittings are now concentrated there. Seaton Deleval's farm buildings cluster around a duck pond and the Norman parish church, dedicated in 1102, was the private chapel of the Delaval family and anyone wishing to see the interior must visit when services are in progress, but this is no bad thing as the hymns do add atmosphere to the building.

Cramlington is a typical new town, but its Thursday market is still focused around the ancient centre of Smithy Square, and is both colourful and comprehensive. Families touring the area will find the Concordia Leisure Centre ideal for the children. There is a large heated swimming pool and plenty of sports facilities. The authorities have succeeded in developing a town built around the core of the ancient village with its typical green still intact. The name Cramlington derives from the

Scandinavian 'Kramel' meaning 'the chief', 'ing' meaning 'kin' and 'ton' meaning enclosure.

This ability to combine the best of the ancient and the modern is not only typical of Cramlington in particular but of Northumberland in general.

CHAPTER 6

Around Rothbury and the River Coquet

Our first introduction to Rothbury was on a truly horrible day in April with freezing rain driving off the hills and we had not time to stop. It looked interesting. The next time we saw the old town, which is pleased to call itself the capital of Coquetdale, was on a glorious May morning with the trees lining the main street in full blossom. It looked beautiful. Any town which is both beautiful and interesting demands a long visit, especially when surrounded by glorious countryside and fascinating attractions, including Brinkburn Priory, Cragside House and Country Park, plus the Coquet Bird Park. These days Rothbury is a base for walkers, fishermen, bird watchers and pony treckers, and has replaced the glory days of the town as a health resort with scores of visitors in search of long life poured in. The attraction was not water but cheese. Not from cows' milk but goats' whey, which was consumed in vast quantities. The good fresh air which was always part of the treatment still remains. Rothbury's market charter goes back to 1205 and was granted by King John ten years before he was forced by his barons to sign the Magna Carta. The road down which he travelled was first called the 'route de Roc' which has now been mis-translated as 'Rotten Row' because of the Englishman's refusal to pronounce Norman French. The history of the area, however, can be traced well beyond this time, and up to the surrounding hills, especially Simonside Ridge, are the remains of an Iron Age fort, several Bronze Age burial sites and some cup and ring shaped carvings scraped into the sandstone rocks. These hills are seen at their best from the B6341 road to Alnwick. Details of the town and the surrounding area can be obtained from the Information Centre, close to which is an interesting old doorway and the parish church. Whilst preparing to gather troops for the fateful 1715 rebellion Lord Derwentwater stayed at the Three Half Moon's Inn. Alas, the hostelry has now gone, but the old doorway remains and a plaque recording the fateful recruiting visit is set into the wall.

The church is dedicated not to one but to All Saints. Its ancient origins are proved by the impressive fragment of a Saxon cross which now serves as the pedestal of a font. It is possible to see on its north side a carving depicting the Ascension and which scholars have dated to around AD 800, and therefore the earliest of its type to be found in Britain. Although the chancel is pure 13th century the rest of the church is a rather plain rebuild of 1850. The furnishings include wood carvings, a pulpit and a screen, all the gifts of Lord Armstrong of Cragside. A firmer connection with the past is the attractive bridge spanning the Coquet, which was built in the 16th century. Although it has obviously had to be repaired since, three of the four ribbed arches are obviously original. The initials W. O. and the date 1759 indicate that the bridge, originally a narrow packhorse span, was widened at this time by a local mason named William Oliphant. As road traffic increased during the present century a further widening was essential but more of its character has been retained than was the case when church was forced into the 19th century.

Brinkburn Priory is open daily between Good Friday or 1st April (whichever is earlier) to 30 September between 10 a.m. to 6 p.m., and situated almost five miles to the south east of Rothbury on the B6334. Administered by English Heritage, Brinkburn has a spacious car park and a pleasant cafe. There is a walk from the car park down to the Coquet through woodlands certain to delight botanists, and in July we identified woodruff, figwort, red campion, bugle and foxglove, but there would be other interesting flowers in spring, and there are goodly numbers of ancient trees including some gnarled old oaks. Rhododendrons are also a feature of the area close to a bend in the river. Brinkburn was founded in 1135 by the Augustinians and its church, built about 1200, is still in use as a church, although services are not regular. When Henry VIII dissolved the Priory in the late 1530s, the local folk were able to petition for the retention of the church. It became their parish church which they dedicated to St Peter and St Paul. Obviously the Augustinians had to go and its new lay governors allowed a house to be constructed on the site. Little maintenance work seems to have been carried out and it was not used for services after 1683, although burials continued. In 1857 the Cadogan family, who lived in the house, employed Thomas Austin, a Newcastle architect, to restore the church. Once the family left the house the site became once more decayed and it was left to the state; but now of course English Heritage to maintain this important site.

Cragside is a complete contrast, being a great Victorian house situated one mile to the north of Rothbury. It was designed on a then open hillside for the first Lord Armstrong by the architect Richard Norman Shaw, and was the first house in the world to be lit by hydroelectricity. The house is open from 1 April to 31 October daily except Mondays, unless it is a Bank Holiday, from 1 p.m. to 5.30 p.m., although the last admission is at 5 p.m. The Country Park which surrounds the house is open from 1 April to 31 October daily from 10.30 a.m. to 7 p.m. or dusk, whichever is earlier. Between November and March, and also on Saturdays and Sundays, the opening times are from 10.30 a.m. to 4 p.m. There is an excellent visitors' centre, entrance to which is covered by the fee payable for either the country park or the house. There are good facilities for the disabled, and the Vickers Rooms Restaurant is a reminder of the first owners' fortune, based on the armaments industry of Vickers Armstrong which, as we described in the introduction, first brought Newcastle in particular and Northumberland in general to our attention. Cragside is a fine tribute to the inventive life of Lord Armstrong who developed his own hydroelectric system within the grounds, which involved the construction of lakes, waterfalls and hydraulic and hydro-electric machinery, all of which had to be designed from first principles. Here then, surrounded by a country park, is an open-air physics laboratory. Now under the care of the National Trust, the original material has been restored and a so-called 'Power Circuit' walk has been laid out in the park. In total there are some 40 miles of walks, but thank goodness the power circuit is much more energy efficient. The original garden has also been restored and planted, and millions of trees and rhododendrons are beautiful at their peak. In 1990 the Armstrong Energy Centre came on stream and this is a tribute to Lord Armstrong's inventions and the part he played in keeping Britain's military strength ahead of its dangerous rivals. The grounds, especially the lakes in winter, are fast becoming popular with wildfowl.

The summer of 1990 saw the establishment of the Coquet Bird Park at Weldon Bridge near Longframlington. This is open from 9 a.m. until dusk throughout the year. On display are more than one hundred rare species of bird including ducks, geese, hens, canaries, finches, rheas, pea-fowl, guinea fowl and the ever popular owls and diurnal birds of prey. The centre also sells young pure-bred birds and welcomes artists and photographers. There is an enclosure where children can walk amongst small animals, an adventure playground, a woodland walk close to the River Coquet, picnic areas, a gift shop and a tea room. The Bird Park should not be rushed for here is a full day's enjoyment at a very reasonable price.

At nearby Longframlington is the Burleigh Factory on Rothbury Road where traditional Northumbrian smallpipes are made and there is also a fascinating display of the history of piping. Those who wish to take away a lasting reminder of the haunting music can buy tapes and if they are lucky they might even persuade the owners to play a tune whilst their guests enjoy a cup of coffee. The 'music centre' is usually open during the week, but for those who want to be sure of expert attention are encouraged to ring Rothbury 50283 or 066 570 635.

Apart from the above areas reached best by car Rothbury makes a fine centre for a walking holiday with visits to the Thrum, Newtown Park and Old Rothbury. All these areas are grouped under the all-embracing name of Rothbury Forest, but there are areas of purple heather on which wild honey bees are found, along with the adults and caterpillars of the Emperor moth. To the west of the town the valley of the Coquet is wide but then it tumbles over a cascade of waterfalls and is then squeezed into a rocky channel which sounds like the Strid at Bolton Abbey in Wharfedale, and which we described in our *Discovering the Yorkshire Dales*. The local name for this turbulent area of squeezed white water is the Thrum, and after rain it is some 200 feet (61 metres) of roaring torrent. To the south of Rothbury is Newton Park which was enclosed round 1275 by Robert Rogerson and although most of the wall has gone some sections do remain, especially between Tosson and Lordenshaw.

The fortified bridge over the river Coquet with Warkworth Castle in the background.

At this time there was nothing decorative about deer parks – they were purely practical collections of deer which were confined until required for the table. Cattle were then much more difficult to overwinter and were more important for their milk than for their flesh. Venison was the main source of fresh meat. At the Lordenshaw end of the deerpark is an example of a prehistoric contour fort built on a prominent spur of land at an ancient crossroads and within it the outlines of primitve dwellings can be delineated.

Other earthworks are found across the valley, especially Old Rothbury, from which there are some of the finest views of both Simonside fells and the Cheviots. Rothbury thus deserves its claim to be the capital of Coquetdale, and from it the source of the Coquet is easily reached via Harbottle and Holystone.

Harbottle Castle in its day was a vitally important stronghold built at the joint expense of Henry II and the Bishop of Durham in 1160. Although now a sparse ruin, it played its part in history as it was here that the grandmother of James I of England was born in 1515. Stone from this building was used in the 17th century to build a 'modern castle'. There is good walking from Harbottle up to the hills which shelter Linsheels Lake and Harbottle Lough.

Holystone is a pretty village with a great religious tradition, although this is sandwiched between two periods of military activity. The Romans had a fort at High Rochester and their legions marched along a road through Holystone and may have stopped to use the well. Around AD 627 Paulinus is said to have baptised 3,000 Northumbrians in the well, now surrounded by stone and with a cross in the centre and maintained by the National Trust. Whether this figure is exaggerated or not it is impossible to say but there was a priory of Augustinian nuns here between the 12th and 16th centuries which no doubt raised revenue from the well. All that remains of this religious house is now the parish church of St Mary which was substantially restored in the 19th century. For most of the time Holystone is still a peaceful village, but occasionally its military history comes full circle, as military manoeuvres are very much a future of Northumberland's open countryside.

From Rothbury the Coquet winds its peaceful way to Warkworth before reaching the sea at Amble. Whenever one is discovering a new county there is no better feeling than getting lost on a glorious June evening whilst searching for somewhere pleasant to stay. This is how we found the Hermitage Hotel in the centre of Warkworth. This was pure serendipidy for we had discovered one of Britain's most beautiful villages complete with ancient castle and Norman church, plus one of the finest fortified bridges ever to be built. All these features are enfolded with a protective loop of the River Coquet. This is Hotspur country, that tough but impetuous member of the Percy family whose castle here was featured in Shakespeare's Henry IV. By the time the Normans arrived a Saxon settlement already existed and was known as Warcewode. No doubt the mound on which the castle stands has been occupied since man settled the area. In AD 738 the settlement plus its Saxon church was given to the monks of Lindisfarne by the King of Northumbria. Werc was apparently the name of the abbess who gave the linen shroud in which the Venerable Bede was buried in the 7th century and Worth was Anglo-Saxon for a fenced enclosure.

The views from the bridge over the Coquet at Warkworth have changed little since the middle ages.

The present castle is a typical Norman structure basically cruciform and built from the 12th century onwards, increasing in size and strength as the Percy family increased in wealth and influence. The family were so strong and confident that it was at Warkworth that the 3rd Earl Percy along with his son Harry whose headstrong temperament earned him the name of Hotspur, plotted to place Henry IV on the throne of England. This came to pass in the final year of the 14th century, and was an ideal theme for an adventure story. No one selected these themes better than Shakespeare and no fewer than three scenes of his play were set at Warkworth. The castle remained the home of the Percys until the 16th century, whilst the fortress at Alnwick was used purely as their main defensive base into which they moved in time of trouble. The Duke of Northumberland still owns the ruins of the castle, although it is open daily and is maintained by English Heritage and there is an entrance fee. The main reason that the castle looks so well is that it was restored in the mid 19th century by none other than the Victorian architect Salvin. For a time Warkworth was a typical Victorian residence set among earlier ruins which thankfully were left undisturbed. The attractive guidebook is entitled

Warkworth Castle and Hermitage, and the latter is one of the most romantic buildings we have ever seen, perhaps because it is so difficult to reach. It can be visited by following a steep footpath from the castle car park which leads through lovely woodlands overlooking the River Coquet. The 14th-century little chapel is then reached by a row-boat ferry which only operates during the season. A narrow winding path passes the Hermit's Spring, usually dry these days, before approaching the chapel which was literally hewn out of the rock which can only be reached via the interesting route described. Initially only three chambers were hacked into the rock above the Coquet, and in the late 14th and early 15th centuries a much more comfortable abode was constructed – were the later hermits a little softer than the pioneers we wonder? There was even a kitchen and a substantial fireplace. Normally such positions were occupied by anchorites, who were religious men who never left their cell, being anchored to their very simple and austere base. The Warkworth Hermitage was different, probably established by the Percys, but few written records are available on which to base a factual account. There is a record dated 1487 which mentions that the fourth Earl of Northumberland appointed Thomas Barker for life to act as 'chaplain of the chantry in Sunderland park'. His function was to celebrate mass in the chapel and his salary was the quite considerable sum of 66s 8d (£3.33). In 1515 we find that Edward Slegg was in charge of Holy Trinity chapel and this time his salary was to be 5 marks, which in modern terms is also £3.33. The area referred to as Sunderland is the land on the bank of the Coquet.

In 1531 Sir George Lancastre was in charge and the sixth earl raised his salary to 20 marks (£13.32) plus pasture for 12 cattle, 2 horses and 1 bull, plus two loads of wood and a supply of fish to be delivered each Sunday. By 1567, however, the hermitage was no longer occupied, and since then the house has fallen into ruin but the chapel itself has fortunately been maintained. Its beauty is enhanced by the fact that it is reached from the River Coquet, which is a delight hereabouts, and there is a lovely walk along the bank from the centre of Warkworth. In the summer swallows swoop low and catch insects hovering over the usually slow-moving water and the bank is lined with trees, including hawthorn, elder and rowan. In the summer

Warkworth's Norman church viewed from the town square.

rowing boats can be hired. It is worth spending time on the river, for here are magnificent views of the castle. There is another walk from the village downstream to one of the best examples of a fortified medieval bridge. It was built around 1379 and the bridge tower is the only one to be found in Northumberland. The view upstream from the bridge is truly beautiful, with the parish church reflected in the water, which is often tinged green with the seaweeds washed in from the nearby estuary. Beneath the bridge is a breeding colony of house martins whose white rumps flash in the sunlight. What a great pity that the view downstream is spoiled by a plain but functional road bridge built in 1965. We found it very strange that there is now an active campaign in motion in support of a bypass road for Warkworth, residents feeling that heavy lorries are causing damage to buildings. One sensible local shopkeeper pointed out to us that all that is needed is to demolish the modern bridge and go back to the situation where light traffic entered the village near the castle, but through traffic would be discouraged. Any exploration of Warkworth should be completed by looking up the main street from the car park, which provides an excellent view of the castle. Overlooking the parked cars on the square is the parish church of St Lawrence which has retained many of its Norman features. Strange as it may seem the church has seen more serious action than the castle. Established in AD 737, St Lawrence, then probably a wooden structure, was destroyed by the Danes in AD 875 and then replaced by a stone structure. Remnants of Saxon crosses remain in the present church. Tragedy struck again on 13 July 1174 when Duncan, the bloodthirsty Earl of Fife, along with the Scottish King, William the Lion, stormed Warkworth, fired the town, and butchered around 300 people who had taken sanctuary in the church, No wonder the present church is a fine example of a dual function house – religious and protective. The thick walls and narrow windows are typical of this design.

Throughout this account of Warkworth we have referred to it as a village, but there is no doubt that it was once a market town; indeed it was here that the Old Pretender was first proclaimed as the rightful King of England in 1715. This took place in the square on 9 October 1715.

Present-day Warkworth, however, is much more peaceful, and will be even more so if the demanded bypass is allowed, which is more likely than the demolition of the 1965 bridge! There is yet another delightful walk from the new bridge down to the estuary of the Coquet, on which lies the town of Amble.

During the late 1980s and early 1990s the fishing port of Amble entertained a visitor who soon assumed the status of a legend. Freddie the Dolphin had booked his place in Northumbrian history. In June 1991 we were lucky enough to be invited by the BBC to present a film for children about Freddie. It had been discovered that he had chosen to swim with human divers, a feature which Dr Horace Dobbs told us has also happened in other parts of the world. Normally, however, the bottle-nosed dolphin lives in groups of around 10 to 15, known as 'schools'. At one time dolphins were much more common, but there numbers have been reduced by pollution and other factors.

Freddie is a bottle-nosed dolphin, *Tursiops truncatus*. The species is distributed throughout the world and although it prefers warm waters it is still fairly abundant along the western shores of the Atlantic. At maturity they can be anything from 9 to 13 feet (3 to 4 metres) long. The upper surface is almost black and this gradually fades until the underparts are white. This is an example of what is known as counter-shading. This means that prey looking down at the dolphin sees a dark back against the dark deep sea, whilst those below see the white belly camouflaged against the light of the sky above the waves. As befits active mammals dolphins spend much of their time feeding and eat cuttlefish, crustaceans and especially small species of fish such as pilchards, mackerel and herring. Dolphins themselves have their own predators to look out for, including sharks and killer whales. The bottle-nosed dolphin also has a prominent dorsal fin which can scare those brought up on films like 'jaws', but unlike sharks they are more of a friend than an enemy of man, and their mouth, although armed with 20 to 26 sharp teeth seems to be set into a friendly grin. Bottle-nosed dolphins seem more inclinded than the common dolphin *Delphinus delphis* to spend time along the shallow coasts and around harbours, and whilst they are usually seen in schools of between 10 and 15 there are several records of animals like Freddie who prefer a solitary life, whilst allowing themselves a few chosen human friends.

Breeding is a gentle and surprisingly loving process which one would expect from such an intelligent species. The gestation period lasts approximately one year, with the female isolating herself from the rest of the school prior to giving birth. Surprisingly she will often allow a second female to attend the birth and perform the function of a midwife. Birth takes between half an hour and two hours and the calf usually emerges tail first. Being mammals it is essential that the female breaks the umbilical cord quickly and gets her baby to the surface and supervises its first breath. The baby relies on its mother's milk for around eighteen months and it is usual

Freddie — Amble's friendly Dolphin comes up for a breath of air and to have his nose tickled.

for the midwife to stay in contact throughout this period. It is normal for only one calf to be born but there are records of twins. The youngster when born is approximately one-third of its mother's length, but the head is large in proportion to the body. Dolphins are fairly long-lived and can expect a span of more than 30 years. The time will come when Freddie will no longer be a part of Amble's life, but by that time he will have given the local tourist industry a well-needed but much deserved boost, and this would be a fitting tribute to his friendly memory.

As we watched Freddie join Horace in the water it was obvious that this was not a zoo and the relationship was on the dolphin's terms. Apparently there are swimmers he likes and will play with, whilst other folk do not appeal to him and he ignores them and slides away to join another diver or perhaps to follow a boat leaving the harbour mouth. A very interesting development involved the work of the stress therapist, Pat Morrell, who is of the opinion that people undergoing problems in their life are relaxed by being in contact with animals, and she had found Freddie to be especially friendly with such people. Autistic children laughed with delight when introduced to Freddie who always seemed to be able to put on a display for his guests.

Whilst Freddie is Amble's most famous son of recent years the delightful little fishing port can certainly guarantee 'life after dolphin'. Not too long ago Amble harbour was crammed with ships onto which coal was loaded from more than 80 mine shafts between the quay and Hauxley only about a mile away. It was a rough town in those days and it was said that young men used to keep on their colliers' clothes rather than venture into the hostelries and appear 'ponced up' and open to rough horseplay. For a few days before we made our film the sea had been rough and all along the attractive little beach adjoining the harbour was a drift line of coal dust. The sea is now mainly clean and Amble-by-the-Sea is an apt name for a coastline designated as an area of outstanding natural beauty. Along the estuary of the River Coquet a marina has been constructed using the old coal staithes as a base. This has been so successful that the complex has twice won a European environmental award. There are a number of caravan sites in the area, and visitors can often be seen watching for the fishing cobles to land their catch of fish. There is nothing like fresh fish for those on a self-catering holiday. Nearby is Druridge Bay Country Park which has been constructed on reclaimed land from the old coal mines. There is some splendid birdwatching in the area all through the year with wintering wildfowl, autumn waders, spring landfalls of migrating species and summer-breeding seabirds on the offshore island of Coquet. Boat trips run from Amble harbour around Coquet island which is now owned by the Royal Society for the Protection of Birds and no landing is permitted. Although we are both keen naturalists we quite agree with keeping all human visitors at bay because here breed thousands of seabirds including fulmar, eider and terns, especially Britain's rarest seabird, the Roseate tern. The lighthouse on the island is now controlled by a mainland computer, and so Coquet is strictly for the birds and we are quite happy to view it from the sand dunes around the Granary area of Amble. On the island there are also the ruins of a Benedictine monastery, or perhaps more of a hermit's cell, dating to the 12th century. We are equally happy to visit Freddie because we, like all his other visitors, arrive on his terms, and he can leave anytime he wants. We once bought fresh fish from the harbour and found enough driftwood on the nearby deserted

Amble, once an industrial port, is now a haven for both fishing craft and pleasure boats.

beach to light a fire and roast our lunch. From our picnic spot among the dunes we watched a fishing boat put out to sea only to be followed by — guess who? — Freddie the Dolphin!

Those bitten by the natural history bug should visit the information centre at Amble and read details of two other nature reserves at Newton and at Hauxley. Also at the information centre is an exhibition telling the story of the history and natural history of Amble. The flowers growing on the sand dunes include the magnificent bloody cranesbill, *Geranium sangujineum*, which is at its best during July and August. The fruit of the plant is shaped like the bill of a heron or a crane, and this accounts for its common English name. Among the birds fishing in the estuary we watched a grey heron catching fish, and also a sandwich tern from Coquet island diving into the sea to catch small fish on which to feed its young. The history of Amble has been traced back to the Bronze Age, and until the coal mines developed in the 19th century it remained little more than a fishing village on the estuary of the Coquet. In recent years its face lift has restored its beauty. Freddie attracted many visitors but the town itself persuades them to stay longer and return soon.

Just south of Amble is Druridge Bay which has five miles of sand fringed by a long line of dunes rich in flowers similar to those at Amble. The area is owned by the National Trust and there are many idyllic spots to park on payment of a small fee. This really is a pretty spot but this has not always been the case as there was once open-cast mining here, but these have been skilfully grassed over. As part of the Druridge Bay project Cresswell Pond Nature Trail was developed during 1991 and was funded by the Countryside Commission as a UK Community Programme. Bird hides are provided overlooking a pond and walks are laid out through the dunes. Information is available from Alcon Farms Visitors' Centre, Blakemoor Farm, Cresswell (Tel. Morpeth 861855).

The Coquet is one of the prettiest rivers in the North Country but it has plenty of rivals including the Aln and the Tweed.

CHAPTER 7

Around Alnwick and its River

The Aln rises on the green hills above the isolated little hamlet of Alnham, before flowing through Whittingham. All that remains at Alnham is the site of a castle, a charming little church and a private house, once a vicarage built in 1541 around a 14th-century pele tower. All round Alnham are sweeping hills which are the catchment area for the river but also offer the walker a goodly number of earthworks and ancient British camps. Alnham was important some 300 years ago when it stood at the crossroads of packhorse and drove roads to and from Scotland and several border settlements. We arrived at Alnham at the end of a heavy rainstorm and just as a rainbow was forming over the green fields, with shafts of sunlight glistening on the grass which was being cropped by Cheviot sheep, the thick wool around their shoulders being very reminiscent of an Elizabethan ruff. Close to the church we found the foundations of the castle which was either demolished or burnt down in 1532. The church of St Michael and All Angels was so skilfully restored in the 1960s that it has retained all its ancient features and appears as if it has been undisturbed for centuries. The arch leading into the chancel is pure 12th century and the timber ceiling gives the impression of solid strength but without losing its attractiveness. On the floor of the chancel are a number of medieval coffin lids and there is also an example of the work of a mason who, in 1611, seems to have grown tired. He was carving the merits of one George Adder and completed only just over half of the job when he added 'and so forth' and left his work. So beautiful and unspoiled is the countryside around Alnham that we feel our task is also unfinished. What a good excuse to return and enjoy a day of birdwatching among the curlew, redshank, lapwing, skylark, meadow pipit, and the summer visiting wheatear.

Whittingham is an attractive little village with a steeply sloping green separated from the parish church of St Bartholomew by the River Aln. Despite this the Vale of Whittingham is often described as being part of Coquetdale. Just off the green is a 15th-century pele tower which dominates more modern housing and is alas no longer used. It is recorded in 1415 as being constructed for Lord Ravensworth of Eslington, and in 1845 it was converted by Lady Ravensworth into an almshouse — an event commemorated by a plaque which reads: 'By the munificence and piety of Lady Ravensworth, this ancient tower, which was formerly used by the villagers as a place of refuge in times of rapine and insecurity, was repaired and otherwise embellished for the use of the deserving poor. AD 1845.' In 1765 Henry Ogle was born in the tower and despite being the inventor of the reaping machine he died in the workhouse at Alnwick in 1848.

There has been a church at Whittingham from the time of King Ceowulf in AD 737 and a little of the Saxon stonework remains on the lower section of the west wall. There was a Norman church dated to 1122 when Henry I gave the living to the Augustinian Canons of Carlisle, and the Dean and Chapter of the Cumbrian border city have retained this to the present day. Towards the end of the 12th century a new chancel was built and a narrow south aisle and arcade were added in the following century — both still important features of the present church. There was probably a chantry chapel here in the 13th century, funded by the Eslingtons, and there is evidence of this, both physical and documentary. An early English piscina set into the south wall suggests that the chantry chapel was here. In 1547, on the order of Henry VIII, all chantry chapels which were Roman Catholic in origin were dissolved, but around 1556 Mary Tudor restored some of these. She allowed Sir Robert Collingwood of Eslington to order 'the erection of a cantaria for a priest to celebrate in the parish church of Whittingham at the Altar of Saint Peter'. Elizabeth I soon reversed such Popery and the revival of chantries was very short-lived indeed. In the 17th century the ravages of time had affected the fabric and the 13th-century south porch was rebuilt. At the same time the attractive sundial was set into the porch. Further remedial work was required in 1839–40 and the top portion of the tower was rebuilt and rather unnecessary pinnacles were added. It is difficult to criticise what happened so long ago but it does seem a pity that the Norman north-aisle arcade

Alnwick Castle looks at its best across lush fields full of grazing sheep.

was removed. In 1870–71 the chancel had to be rebuilt and the old walls supported by buttresses, the work being funded by the Dean and Chapter of Carlisle with generous help from Lord Ravensworth.

Whittingham means 'the dwelling in the white meadow', and its importance was due to its strategic position of fords over the river and at the junction of the road from Alnwick with that running from Newcastle to Edinburgh. Whittingham village can claim to have been cheated of two claims to fame. Like Almouth it claims to be the place where St Cuthbert was elected Bishop of Lindisfarne. Everyone knows the song of Scarboro Fair but it seems that Whittingham has first claim to this tune.

> Are you going to Whittingham fair?
> Parsley, sage, rosemary and thyme.
> Remember me to one who lives there,
> For once she was a true love of mine.

Whittingham fair was held annually around 29 August and was very much a part of Northumbrian folklore. It is still one of the best places in Britain to hear of traditional border games even though the serious practice is now part of history. Whittingham does have one undisputed claim

concerning Edred, Bishop of Lindisfarne. In AD 800 he
had a vision of St Cuthbert pursuading the Danes to elect as
their leader a boy called Guthred who had been the slave of
a widow of Whittingham. The Danes took the boy to a hillside
called Oswigedune where Edred showed them the coffin of St
Cuthbert. The new leader of the Danes agreed to keep the
peace and actually gave to the Saint all the land between
Tyne and Wear to the east of Hadrian's Wall. How true is
this story? The fact that one named Guthred was crowned
King of Northumbria at Whittingham in AD 883 would suggest
that at least the village has one unchallenged claim to fame.
Although not open to the public there is an attractive pele-based
dwelling two miles to the south-west of Whittingham at Callaly
Castle. This is an early pele built in the 13th century onto which
a 17th-century mansion was skilfully dovetailed.

We love Alnwick. We must do, as when we looked through
our travel diaries we found that on our first seven visits to
the old town it rained except for one day in March —
on this day it snowed! There have been eleven subsequent
visits, and each has seen some sunshine, so perhaps we were
right to persevere. Alnwick is rightly regarded as the second
town of Northumberland, but unlike Newcastle it has been
almost untouched by industry since the 19th century. If coach
travellers could be brought back from the Turnpike Age they
would clatter through the Hotspur Gate and recognise the
same hostelries. The menu would differ but the food is just
as wholesome. One more recent piece of history is found in
the ballroom of the White Swan hotel which was removed from
the ocean liner Olympic, the sister ship of the ill-fated Titanic,
which was broken up at Wallsend. Each Shrove Tuesday a fierce
football game is played with no limits on team size and as far as
we can see no rules. Anyone who loves fishing should visit the
Hardy fishing museum on the edge of the town.

Any account of Alnwick should begin by a visit to the Castle
which opens from May to September from 1 p.m. to 5 p.m. each
day except Saturdays, but during bank holidays it also opens on
Saturday. The histories of the Castle and of Northumberland
are inseparable, the structure being attractive from whatever
angle it is seen, including the air. Our favourite approach is
along a footpath which follows a deep winding loop of the

The best approach to Alnwick is through a narrow arch of the Hotspur gate.

River Aln and across lush green fields on which graze sheep and cattle. Alnwick castle dates to the late 11th century when Yvo de Vesey, who was appointed as the first Norman Baron, set about constructing a border fortress. He and subsequent owners, especially the Percy family, certainly succeeded. The fact that it has been a private home since its establishment means that Alnwick is a solid chunk of living history as opposed to a very attractive ruin, a fate which befell most of the Northumberland castles. The last of the de Vesey line died in 1297, but the castle was left in trust for an illegitimate son. The Bishop of Durham was supposed to be a reliable trustee, but it seems that he sold the estate and used the money for his own purposes. In 1309 Henry Percy took up residence and it was he and his descendants who created an invincible border fortress at a time when only the strongest survived. Following the union of England and Scotland in 1603 such fortresses were redundant and Alnwick during the following couple of centuries became almost derelict. In the 18th century the first Duke of Northumberland carried out an impressive restoration, employing James Payne and Robert Adam. In the mid 19th century the 4th Duke almost gutted the interior to produce a Victorian country house and much of Adam's work was unfortunately ripped out to make room for Anthony Salvin's flair for the Italian Renaissance style. The furnishings are, however, stunning, with collections of Meisen china and works of art by Titian, Van Dyke and Canaletto, the latter obviously purchased to blend with Salvin's Italian design. A fine example of Canaletto shows Sion House on the Thames at Brentford painted in 1752. Once the abbey of Benedictine nuns, but which had been a Percy home from the time of Queen Elizabeth, Sion House was restored by Robert Adam in the 1760s. Works by other Italian artists on display include the *Visitation*, part of a Fresco by Sebastiano del Piomb, and the *Lady with a Lute* by Palma Vecchi. Although the interior of the house has been extensively changed over the centuries the exterior has not been altered much and Alnwick is still very much a well maintained medieval fortress, one of the most spectacular castles to be found anywhere in Britain. Here is history writ large in stone! They tell of the history of the Percy's and of England. The family reached England as part of the entourage of William the Conqueror, their roots being in and around the Normandy village of Percée. The name means 'a clearing in a wood'. Sir Henry de Percy was the first of the family to own Alnwick, and it was in the early years of the 14th century that the stout keep was constructed along with the constable's towers and the impressive postern. Whether the Percys were warlike by nature or whether they were influenced by the conflicts typical of border areas it is hard to say. In any event every male Percy was a doughty fighter and whenever the borders were quiet

The harbour, a gift of the Craster family, to the village which bears their name.

they went off to fight on the Continent. Such a family would be bound to attract legend as well as embroidered fact, and it is said that the Order of the Garter had its origins in these parts in 1349 when Edward III was on the throne. The King and his army were camped around Wark castle on Tweedside and a ball was held in his honour. The Countess of Salisbury, whilst dancing, lost her garter, which caused her embarrassment but was a source of amusement to others. The gallant King raised the garter and said 'Honi soit qui mal y pense' — 'Evil be to he who evil thinks'. The order of the garter was thus originated — what a pity that this cannot be proved. If this is totally legend then the exploits of Harry Hotspur, the son of the first Earl, are at least partly true. From the time that the 12-year-old gained praise for his behaviour during the siege of Berwick to his death on the battlefield at Shrewsbury in 1403 he was a fiersome soldier, always at odds with the equally fierce Douglas family based on the Scots' side of the border. The two met at Otterburn in an encounter described in Chapter 4 and by Sir Walter Scott who tells of the Douglas's premonition that he would die:

> 'But I hae dreamed a dreary dream
> Beyond the Isle of Skye,
> I saw a dead man win a fight
> And I think that man was I.

Many years ago we saw a film called *The Man Who Never Was* based on a Second World War intelligence operation involving planting a corpse in the sea to be discovered by the Germans and with papers on him to indicate an incorrect landing point for an invasion. It begins with the above four lines and these took our thoughts back to Otterburn, to Hotspur's castles at Warkworth and of course Alnwick. If they were lucky in war the Earls of Northumbria had periods when they were unlucky in love, none more sad than the plight of Henry the sixth earl who was in love with Anne Boleyn who was then being pursued by a much more powerful Henry, King of England. The seventh earl was even more unfortunate as he supported the claim of Mary Queen of Scots much to the annoyance of Elizabeth. Thomas Percy nailed the Scot's colours so firmly to his mast during the Rising of the North that in 1572 he was beheaded. He left his mark on the structure of Alnwick Castle, but what improvements were made were doomed to crumble away following the family's implication in the Gunpowder Plot of 1605. Henry Percy, who dabbled in alchemy, was known as

Girls at Craster working hard on gutting the herring ready for the kippering process. This photograph was taken in the 1890's.

the 'Wizard Earl' and was imprisoned in the Tower of London for 15 years despite continually pleading his innocence. In 1670 the Percy family, at least on the male side, came to an end with the death in Turin of the 11th Earl of Northumberland. He did, however, leave a daughter who married the Proud Duke of Somerset. It was Elizabeth their granddaughter who married a Yorkshire baronet who was instrumental in reviving Alnwick and the Northumberland estates. Sir Hugh Smithson changed his name to Percy and in 1750 became the Earl of Northumberland, being given a Dukedom 16 years later. The kiss of life was about to be administered and the estate is still alive and well, safe in the hands of the descendants of Sir Hugh and his lady, Elizabeth. The improvements made to Alnwick have been described already, but the extensive grounds also received considerable attention. The grounds are also open to the public and even if a full day was allowed the 'Windsor of the North' would still withhold many secrets. The grounds known as Hulne Park, are surrounded by some nine miles of wall and

were laid out by Lancelot Brown, a Northumbrian, who well
earned his name of Capability and whose life is described in
Chapter 5.

The park wraps around the edge of the town, like a
comfortable blanket, and contains the ruins of a priory,
and abbey and a most remarkable folly. Hulne Priory was a
Carmelite house established around 1240 and the Whitefriars
have left behind a ruin of sufficient magnitude to enable its
basic features to be realised. The original defensive wall and the
tower built in 1488 are the most interesting features, but few
ruins can be sited in such a pleasant and undeveloped setting.
The only blot on the landscape hereabouts is an 18th-century
shooting tower. Down on the Aln are the remains of the Priory
fish ponds and scholars have been able to identify the sites of
domestic offices, a mill, a brewhouse and a bakery.

Alnwick abbey is nearer to the town and is reached via a
bridge from Canongate and thence to the abbey lodge. This
was founded for Premonstatensian Canons, who also dressed
in white habits, the ground being given by Eustace Fitz-John
and his wife Beatrice. Originally the abbey was outside the
castle grounds and has only been absorbed in the last 200
years. It was, however, a wealthy establishment, no doubt
benefiting from the protection afforded by the sheer presence
of the castle. This may account for the fact that the history of
Alnwick abbey was not very remarkable — its existence was
far too comfortable. In 1304 a monk wrote a poem in Latin
about Robin Hood, the first literary reference to the hero,
and could it be that Friar Tuck was a Northumbrian? After
the abbey was dissolved in 1539 the buildings fell into ruin, a
process accelerated by the locals who used it as an unofficial
but easily accessible quarry. The presence of a priory and an
abbey begs the question as to whether there was any contact
between the two. Beyond Monks Bridge is a site known as the
'Trysting Tree', a gnarled old oak which was thought to be the
meeting point of the two houses. This seems to be a reasonable
suggestion, as the place is half way between the two houses.
The three thousand acres of Hulne Park can best be seen from
Brislee Tower, the first duke's folly designed by Robert Adam.
We feel that 'folly' is a rather insulting term for a 90-foot (27.4
metres) tower which provided work for the local people and

gave the Duke an ideal vantage point from which to survey his own estate. On a good day seven ancient castles could be seen, including Warkworth, Dunstanburgh, Chillingham, Ross and Alnwick itself.

So much for the Castle and its grounds — what of the town itself? Two features are immediately obvious as Alnwick is approached — the Tenantry Column and the Hotspur gate through the arch of which the traffic enters and leaves the town. In the days before the bypass was built this section of the old A1 was a notorious bottleneck. The 83-foot (25.2 metre) high fluted column is not, as has been suggested, another Duke's Folly, but a reminder that the relationship between the town and the castle was at times very friendly although throughout the long history there were bound to have been family arguments. The monument records the military exploits of the 2nd Duke who fought in the American War of Independence. It was built, however, as a result of the conclusion of the Napoleonic wars which resulted in a reduction of farm produce. The Duke reacted by reducing the farm rents by 25 per cent and the column was paid for by the grateful townfolk. To commemorate the opening on 1 July 1816 coins were struck, a single gold being given to the Duke and three of silver to Stevenson the architect, Farrington the artist, and Mrs Pringle, on whose land the column was erected. The twenty-one oldest tenants were given bronze medals and there were also a number of copper coins minted, but historians seem unsure what happened to these. By the time the final touches had been given to the column it was 12 December 1818. Can we believe that the Duke was so surprised that his tenants could afford the monument that he raised their rents again?

The so-called Hotspur gate shows that the relations between town and castle were not always friendly because no walls surrounded Alnwick until 1433 when Henry VI gave permission to enclose it following a number of damaging attacks by the Scots. Despite some writers stating that the Earl paid for the building this was not the case, for he left the townspeople to find the money to protect themselves. Money was not easily found, and it was more than 50 years before the stone encirclement was complete. The Earls of Northumberland made no contribution at all. Four gates were built along the walls: Bondgate to the

The men of Craster working hard on the windlass to pull their fishing boats up onto the beach. The photograph was taken about 1900.

south, Clayport at the south-west, Poltergate protecting the west, and at the north stood Narrowgate. Alas only Bondgate stands at the present time, and this is now usually called Hotspur's Tower, even though the bold knight had been long dead before it was even planned. Credit should be given only where due and Bondgate Tower would be a more accurate name. During the 17th and 18th centuries the three-storeyed structure was sometimes used as a secure prison.

Within its walls the market town must have felt secure, for since its establishment in 1291 Alnwick had proved to be very vulnerable. Market day is on Saturday with early closing on Wednesday, and there is no finer sight than Alnwick early on market day morning as the stallholders prepare for a hectic day of business. The information centre is situated almost in the middle of all this activity. Attractive buildings overlooking the market include the Town Hall of 1771 and the White Swan. In late June or early July Alnwick Fair, held since 1297, takes the town back to the Middle Ages as local folk and visitors alike let their hair down and join in the innocent fun. A walk up into Bailegate connects to the castle to the parish of St Michaels' built in the 15th century, but much altered in the 19th by several architects including Dobson and Salvin. Unlike most Northumbrian churches St Michaels' was built so close to a castle that it was protected. This allowed Henry VI in 1464 to endow the church built in the Perpendicular style but incorporating a few Norman features from an earlier church. A statue of the King is to be found in the baptistry. The spacious chancel is said to have been influenced by the monks of Alnwick abbey. The church was so solidly constructed that the exterior has been largely left unchanged since the 15th century despite the extensive changes carried out inside during Victorian times. Fortunately some intersting monuments have been left intact including two 14th-century tombs, a medieval religious figure and a Flemish carved chest, also from the 14th century, and which would have been part of the furnishings of the earlier Norman church. The site chosen for the building and also for the castle provided panoramic views over the twisting River Aln, surely one of the country's most attractive and historic watercourses. The area around Alnwick once had its share of industry, especially around Shilbottle, which was once a mining village. The coal mines have now gone and the place deserves more visitors than it gets. St James church is attractive and is overlooked by a pele tower once used as the vicarage.

In a coast as beautiful as that of Northumberland it is hard to find somewhere special — and yet we found it. It is called Almouth, set, as its name implies, on the estuary of the River Aln. The port claims to be the place where St Cuthbert was proclaimed Bishop of Lindisfarne at the Great Synod of AD 684. This may or may not be true and the same claim is also made by several other towns and villages of Northumbria, particularly Whittingham. There have, however, been a good number of Saxon artefacts found at Alnmouth and in 1789 a carved cross was dug up on Church hill, but neither this nor the Norman church which followed it exist today. In 1806 a tremendous storm struck Alnmouth, destroyed the old church and altered the course of the river and put an end to one of the area's most important harbours situated on the south side of the town and which has now silted up. When John Wesley

The view of Dunstanburgh Castle across the beach near Craster harbour.

visited the area in 1748 he wrote that Alnmouth was 'a small seaport famous for all kinds of wickedness'. It had served as the port for the important town of Alnwick for centuries and during the 18th and 19th centuries it exported vast volumes of corn. Some of the granaries have been converted into houses with a goodly number of these now offering wholesome bed-and-breakfast accommodation for an expanding tourist industry. Such an important harbour was thought to be important to the American 'pirate' Paul Jones who is said to have fired at the church but missed it exactly by a mile. It seems to us much more likely that he would be firing at the grain warehouses. The church which now overlooks Alnmouth is the third on the site and was built as a result of public subscription, being consecrated on 6th November 1876. It is a typically functional Victorian church and in our last visit two inscriptions took our eye. The church leaflet bade us: 'Be still and know that God is here'. The other told us to resist the ordination of women. We enjoyed one but could have done without the other.

Settlement began early around Alnmouth and the name Aln is Celtic meaning 'bright water', and several Bronze Age and Celtic artefacts have been found in the area. An Anglian settlement was set up by a chieftain named Adda who built an impressive fortress in the area, probably on the site of a Roman settlement which was called Woodchester, but little remains of either fort. Even the gravestone of the Saxon King Eadulph was removed from Castle Hill to Alnwick Castle. As the Victorians discovered the value of the seaside, Alnmouth became a popular watering place, and most of this 19th-century genteelness has been retained. The narrow street has good hotels, neat tea and coffee rooms, and some very attractive shops selling gifts, books, maps and postcards. It is the dune fringed beach, however, which is the joy being overlooked by a pleasant nine-hole golf course on which many visitors learn how difficult it can be to drive across an offshore wind. There is an 18-hole golf course at nearby Foxton and the station is only half a mile from the village. Parking in the village is not easy but for a small fee there is plenty of parking among the dunes. A most pleasant walk then leads to the village alongside the golf course with views across the dunes to the expanse of sand to the sea with Coquet island beautiful on a good day, and even on a day of wind and rain, hauntingly attractive.

The coastline to the north of Alnmouth is also a delight and dominated by Craster and Dunstanburgh Castle. We set off to discover Craster and to find the secrets of the English kipper. We found this and much more besides in one of the friendliest villages which sets out its stall to welcome visitors. We parked in the extensive area laid out in an old whinstone quarry above the harbour and on a hot day found a happy welcome both for us and for our black labrador at the Bark Pots Cafe. As we enjoyed crab sandwiches and a pot of good strong tea the owner told us that his father and aunts had been associated with the herring fishing, the making and mending of nets as well as salting and kippering the herring. In the old days the nets were made of cotton or flax and had to be protected from the chemical action of the sea. To keep rotting to a minimum the nets were soaked in tannic acid which was produced by boiling bark in water and thus accounting for the name of the cafe. Here we also have the origin of the surnames of Barker and Tanner.

Stone was exported from the harbour as were salted herring and the kippers which are produced by smoking over oak chippings, but employing a secret and well guarded method. At one time vast quantities of herring were caught around the coast of Britain but a combination of over fishing certainly and pollution probably, reduced their numbers. Our host had many old photographs on the walls of the cafe as a reminder of the good old days of fishing and the stone quarrying industry. He told us of his aunts who, along with many local women, followed

Although long ruined, Dunstanburgh Castle has sufficient remaining to show its rugged strength. A fine example is the Lilburn tower built in 1325.

the migration of the herring which reached northern Scotland early in the spring and then moved down the coast reaching East Anglia in the autumn. The boats followed the fish and rather than waste time returning to home port the fish gutters and salters travelled down the coast and hired huts at various ports in which to process the huge catches. This was more efficient than training local women around the host ports for two week's work each year.

Craster is actually an estate village named after the Craster family: in 1906 the harbour was rebuilt to commemorate the life of a brother who had died in Tibet. These days the herring have gone and nowadays only crabs and lobsters are landed. Kippers are still produced using the traditional method but now the herrings have to be brought in to the village. Visitors are welcome to watch some of the process and adjacent to the kippering sheds is a smashing fish restaurant obviously specialising in fish and especially herring and kippers. In the village is Craster Tower the family home which was built in 1415 but with considerable 18th century alterations. Northumberland is walking country, but it is not always necessary to burst your lungs on the high hills. From Craster harbour one of the prettiest coastal footpaths leads to Embleton and on the way passes the largest ruined castle in the county — Dunstanburgh which dominates the coastline close to Craster and is perched on a 100-foot outcrop above the North Sea. Until 1939 whinstone was exported from Craster and was popular for making street setts. It was quarried from the area now occupied by the car park, but the economy of the village is now firmly based on tourism. Judging by the beauty of the coastal path Craster's future is secure. In 1963 Sir John Craster produced an informative little leaflet entitled *The Natural History of Dunstanburgh Castle Point* and this has inspired us to visit the area on many occasions and at all seasons of the year. We have watched Manx shearwaters and gannets, the latter breeders from the Bass Rock off the coast of North Berwick, battle with the winter storms, an increasing number of fulmars which breed on the cliffs and both arctic and sandwich terns fishing by diving into the calm blue summer sea. We have picnicked among the thrift perhaps better called the sea pink and which was once featured on the pre-decimal coin the threepenny piece. Also

Bamburgh, dominated by its castle, has lots of shops for tourists, overlooking the old village green.

dominant on this area of coast is the purple headed knapweed, the large daisy-like scentless mayweed and the common scurvy grass which was once taken to sea on the water barrels of sailors as a protection against Scurvy caused by a deficiency in Vitamin C which is present in the green fleshy leaves of the plant. This is also insect country and we have seen the common residents the six spot burnet moth and the cinnabar moth both of which have caterpillars which feed upon ragwort with the adults drinking the nectar of yellow stonecrop and purple thyme. We had one exciting day in late August when we saw several painted ladies which are migrant butterflies with orange and black markings and also with white spots on the forewing.

The gloriously varied display of natural history continues to Embleton Bay, but plenty of time should be allowed to explore Dunstanburgh Castle which can only be reached on foot by far the best and easiest way being from Craster. The castle is maintained by English Heritage and stands on National Trust land and an entry fee is payable. The opening hours are from 10 a.m. to 6 p.m. between Good Friday or April 1 whichever is earlier to 30 September. From 1 October to 31 March or

Maunday Thursday the castle opens from Tuesday to Sunday between 10 a.m. and 4 p.m. Dunstanburgh has quite a tale to tell. The walk from Craster soon reveals that the 1906 harbour was constructed on a new site, the original anchorage having been built to serve the castle. You can still see the remains of a once deep and narrow inlet which ran below the southern horn of the crescent shaped site on which Dunstanburgh was built. The old harbour has long been smothered beneath tons of shingle, but once you know it is there the entrance can be imagined, and it can also be seen that it was designed to isolate the castle and produce an island fortress. Few fortresses could be so firmly sited on top of solid basalt made use of by the ancient Britons and also by the Romans. It is thus rather surprising that the early Normans did not build a castle here and Dunstanburgh was only started in 1313 by Thomas Earl of Lancaster who was executed for treason in 1322 whilst the building was in its early stages. The building is unique in Northumberland as it was not built to guard the border as were Norham and Wark-on-Tweed, or to provide a Royal residence whilst the monarch was fighting the Scots as were Newcastle and Bamburgh or even to protect a feudal lord in residence as at Warkworth, Bothal or Alnwick. It seems that Dunstanburgh's function was to defend the port at its feet. Following the death of Thomas the castle passed to John of Gaunt whose practical mind conceived the addition of a magnificent gateway, which still stands flanked by a couple of solid round towers. The castle, or perhaps the port, was a focus of fierce fighting during the Wars of the Roses and Dunstanburgh changed hands five times, each occasion precluded by a fierce bombardment which left it badly damaged at the end of the conflict in the 1480s. By 1538 the weather had caused even further decay and it is recorded that crops of corn and hay were actually being grown within the walls of the castle. Such a well built structure, however, is bound to be a survivor and much remains including John of Gaunt's gatehouse and the Lilburn tower built in 1325 for John Lilburn who was constable at the time and his residence was built on the highest point of the castle enclosure.

Just to the south of Craster near Howick is the so-called Rumbling Churn which is a cavern in the rocks into which the sea drives and turns pebbles in an action similar to the spin drier of a washing machine. It is particularly spectacular on a day of gales and high tides when spumes of water are forced high into the air and the churn does more than rumble — it roars!

Embleton is north of the castle overlooking a splendid bay just to the north of Dunstanburgh. Although often overshadowed by the gems on offer around Craster, there is much to discover in the village and some fascinating scenery and natural history around the bay itself. Holy Trinity church existed in medieval times but it was rather badly restored in the 19th century; the 12th century tower, however, is tunnel vaulted and with magnificent stone arches. The vicarage is built around a pele tower constructed in 1415. Within the church are memorials to the family of Grey of Falloden, one of whom was foreign secretary which was his job and a famous ornithologist which was his love. There is no shortage of sea birds on this wonderful stretch of coast, which always has us debating whether to be naturalists for the day or to spend the time discovering yet more facets of its history. We end up doing both and then deciding to return. This is truly the fascination of Northumberland. There is so much to see and far too little time in which to observe it.

CHAPTER 8

The Northumberland Coast

In contrast to the coastline south of Amble which is recovering from its industrial past, the area northwards from Beadnell has not had to endure too much interference and has long been a popular tourist area. Bearing in mind beauty, history and natural history plus the many acres of open space we feel that this is the most interesting stretch of coast in Britain. We have known this area for many years and have made several television programmes here and have stayed at Chathill, Seahouses, Belford, Bamburgh and on Holy Island. There are two good ways of exploring this area the most obvious being to follow the route of the old A1 and taking periodic diversions to the places of interest. The other, and our favourite, is to follow the coastroad from Embleton, the first stop being at Beadnell. This is now a typical holiday area with lots of caravan parks, beachside shops, cafes and villas offering bed and breakfast accommodation all based on the presence of open expanses of flat sand flanked by sheltering dunes. In the harbour area is the headquarters of the Beadnell Sailing Club and also a castle-like structure which is actually a group of 18th century limekilns which have been preserved by the National Trust. Opposite the kilns is a neat little harbour used by fishing cobles painted blue and white and which specialise in catching lobsters, but especially crabs. The fishermen use the arches of the kilns in which to store their tackle. From the harbour Beadnell Bay sweeps westwards and then turns south with the flat sand giving way to Snoot Point around which there are some interesting rock pools. Newton Links at the southern end of the bay is now National Trust land and ever popular with picnickers and botanists. Beadnell Bay has facilities for an assortment of water sports including sailing and water skiing with the harbour having the distinction of being the only one on the east coast which actually faces west. It is established that there was a settlement here in Saxon times with a chapel dedicated to St Ebba who was the sister of Oswald, the Christian King of Northumbria. Near the harbour is the Craster Arms an inn built around a pele tower. Just inland is the village of Chathill of which the most important feature is Preston Tower. This was built by Sir Robert Harbottle in 1392 and is one of the 78 pele towers in the county which were listed in 1415. This building is a fine example of a pele with the tunnel-vaulted rooms which have altered little since the day they were completed. Two rooms have been furnished in the style of the period and there are also displays of historic and local information. Preston Tower is open all the year round during daylight hours and in our view should be a must for all discoverers of the county.

If the area around Beadnell is quiet then the same cannot be said for Seahouses which is all hustle, bustle, tumult and tourism. There are fish and chips, hamburgers, daft hats and candy floss but all achieved with eminent good taste without any loss in atmosphere. Seahouses is still dominated by its harbour which specialises in fishing and tourist trips out to the Farne Islands.

Early in the 19th century the small fishing village of North Sunderland was enlarged and a new harbour was financed by Lord Crewe anxious to export the products of a developing lime burning industry. It is still possible to locate the old quarries now filled with water and which are to the south of the village. The essential coal required for this process was dug out of shallow mines situated to the north and west of the settlement. This new development at the seaward end of Sunderland became known as Seahouses and the name was probably invented to distinguish it from the Sunderland on Wearside which was fast developing as a ship building town. Seahouses soon developed into a hard working port which also exported corn the ships used being small sailing vessels. Even when the lime quarries had closed and the railways came the harbour evolved by changing its function to serve the herring fishing and curing industry. Many historians think that the first experiments on smoke curing of herring to produce kippers was carried out at Taylor Street, Seahouses. In July and August around the turn of the 20th century drifters, which were usually painted black and had dark sails, put into Seahouses but their home areas included Hebridean, Shetland and Cornish ports. Steamers also headed for Seahouses bringing in cargoes of salt and took away barrels of salted herring destined for Northern Europe. Seahouses is still an active fishing port, but is nowhere nearly so important as it was earlier in the century but the seamens' shortfall in income is more than met by the tourists eager to sail around or to set foot on the Farne Islands. The group is about 10 miles to the south of Berwick-upon-Tweed and is the eastern extremity of the Great Whin Sill a sheet of tough resistant dolerite running almost 80 miles across the north of England and is an important geological feature of Northumberland. From Seahouses the Farnes lie between 1½ to 4¾ miles off shore and depending upon the state of the tide there are between 15 and 20 islands. Two main groups can be recognised, separated by a mile of sea called the Staple Sound and further deliniated by two outliers — the Megstone to the west and the Crumstone to the east. The largest island is the Inner Farne which occupies 16 acres at low water of which 11 acres are bare rock. Other outcrops large enough to be regularly referred to by name are Staple Island, the Brownsmen, the Big Harcar, North and South Wamses, East and West Wideopens and the Longstone. In general the Great Whin Sill slopes south-west to north-east which means that the majority of the islands have steep faces to the south and west and these provide ideal habitat for breeding seabirds. Staple Island is a perfect example of this to the south east of which are the three Pinnacles, columnar flat topped stacks about 19 metres (60 feet) high and weathering has separated them from the main island. On the Inner Farne the cliffs are even higher and may reach 25 metres (80 feet). Whilst the smaller islets are composed mainly of bare rock the more substantial islands are covered with a thick layer of boulder clay on top of which a peaty soil supports a surprisingly lush vegetation. Such islands would be suitable for human settlement especially those in search of peace in troubled times. Biologists feel that, like the rest of Northumberland, the Farnes were once covered in trees and that there were settlements on the larger islands in prehistoric times. There is, however, no proof of this but there is a written record of St Aidan, the first bishop of Lindisfarne from AD 635 and AD 652 travelling out to the Farnes in search of solitude. The most famous resident of the Inner Farne, however, was St Cuthbert who retired to a life of a prayer in AD 676 and it was only with great reluctance that he was persuaded to leave his beloved birds and become Bishop of Lindisfarne in AD 676. After two years Cuthbert felt that his end was near and returned to the Inner Farne where he died on March 20 687. Cuthbert's life style set a trend and the Inner Farne attracted a regular supply of religious hermits. After Cuthbert those who followed were of minor importance but in the 12th century a monk called Bartholomew lived on the Inner Farne for 42 years. In 1255 the Convent of Durham built a small Benedictine house on the island and this continued until 1536 when Henry VIII dissolved it. What Cuthbert would have thought of this house we can but guess but it would not have impressed him to see two monks one called the Master and the other the Associate looked after by two servants in a rather comfortable building. Much of the structure remains including the chapel dedicated to St Cuthbert and which was rebuilt around 1370. By 1848, however, the holy shrine was described as ruinous and would have fallen down had it not been for a restoration funded by the Venerable Charles Thorp who was Archdeacon of Durham between 1831 and 1862. He not only restored the basic stonework but he also sent some oak furnishings from Durham and provided some stained glass for the East Window. Some signs of the chapel of St Mary also remain as does a stone coffin in an enclosure which was hewn to hold the remains of Thomas Sparowe who was master from 1423 to 1431. The castle-like tower also has an interesting history and is thought to stand over the site of St Cuthbert's cell. The structure was built by Prior Castell the Prior of Durham from 1494 to 1519 but during Elizabeth's reign it did actually function as a fort. In the reign of Charles II a licence was granted on December 1 1673 which required a fire to be kept burning on top of the tower at night thus providing the first primitive lighthouse to function on the Farnes. It is doubtful if the lighthouses on the Farnes would have been any more famous than those anywhere else had the SS Forfarshire not floundered in 1838. This led to the heroism of Grace Darling (1815–1842) spreading through the length and breadth of Britain and even beyond. The events of September 7 and the fate of the 400-ton Forfarshire en route from Hull to Dundee was treated by William Darling, the lighthouse keeper on the Longstone lighthouse, as routine and

Few churches are more beautifully sited than Bamburgh with the castle behind as a lovely backdrop.

his entry in the log shows his modesty and neither he nor Grace sought the spotlight of publicity. He wrote 'Nine persons held on by the wreck and were rescued by the Darlings'. He made no mention of their efforts to launch their boat or the skill needed to row it across the rough sea. Grace became a heroine at the age of only 17 but she refused all offers of fortune. One of the offers came from the managers of London's Drury Lane theatre who wanted her to appear on stage as part of an elaborate tableau and to be seen rowing across mountainous waves. Grace refused and remained at home until she died of tuberculosis at the age of only 26. Some literary scholars think that Dickens based his character Lizzie Hexham on Grace and he described her as 'a simple modest young woman with the most amiable look and the sweetest smile, a thoroughly good creature who under a modest exterior hides a spirit capable of the most exalted devotion'. Actually she was probably a down-to-earth, no nonsense, Northumbrian lass who was born and is buried at nearby Bamburgh and who knew the wildlife of the Farnes. Indeed she and her father added to their meagre living by gathering geological specimens, flowers, shells and birds' eggs for the collections of private individuals and museums.

William Darling actually spread sand on areas of bare rock to provide a suitable nesting site for the terns. The Darlings were collectors not butchers but there was a period when so-called sportsmen in the 1870s hired boats and guns and slaughtered the breeding birds perched on the cliffs. This and the local fishermen collecting the eggs for eating could well have caused the extinction of many species had it not been for the passing of the first Bird Protection Act in 1880. Since 1925 the Islands have been owned by the National Trust and the colonies are safe. Organised trips are made around the group and landing is allowed on the Inner Farne, with regular sailings from the harbour at Seahouses. A few years ago the boats used were a little rough and ready, but all this has changed as the age of tourism takes over and gathers momentum. The boats are clean and comfortable the commentary informed and professional and the wildlife on view spectacular. It is the birds which usually grab the headlines especially the huge numbers of puffin, guillemot, razorbill, sandwich, roseate, common and arctic tern plus assorted gulls, fulmar, ringed plover and our own particular favourite the eider duck. This is locally called the 'Cuddy Duck' or St Cuthbert's duck as it was apparently a favourite of the Saint who often waded into the sea up to his neck to contemplate so it is said, the scriptures. We believe he found much solace in watching the wild creatures, especially diving ducks.

Another gem in the crown of the Farnes are the grey seals which are now fortunately protected by law. Although they do take some fish which annoys the fishermen they more than compensate for this by their tourist attraction for here is the only place on the east coast where they breed. There are only two native British seals the common and the grey, the latter being considerably larger the bulls being around 8 foot 6 ins (almost 3 metres) and weighing up to 650 lbs (290 kg). The most prominent feature of the bulls is their huge Roman nose and the thick folds of skin around the neck which is almost reminiscent of an Elizabethan ruff. The calves at birth are around 3 feet (1 metre) in length and weigh around 30 pounds (13.3 kg). The milk of seals is notoriously rich and the young grow very quickly, their pale coats are moulted and they learn to adjust to the sea. The young are born in November and December with the favoured nurseries being the Wamses, Brownsman and Staple Island. Seals can be seen throughout the year and the boatmen seldom fail to provide their passengers with excellent views and photographic opportunities.

There are many publications dealing with the natural history of this area of coastline, but relatively few opportunities to have what is these days referred to as a 'hands on' experience. During the making of a television film we were lucky enough to work with Selby Allen who with his wife Kathlene runs the Marine Life Centre and Fishing Museum just off the harbour at Seahouses. This is open from Easter to the end of September from 10 a.m. to 6 p.m. and in October and November from 10 a.m. to 4 p.m. In the entrance behind a well stocked shop is a display explaining the intricacies of crab and lobster fishing. There is the 'Joan Dixon' a 9 metre (30 foot) long fishing coble which operated for over 40 years from her home port of Beadnell. She only ceased operation in the late 1980s and a video shows her actually at work. Children get the 'hands on' experience in a stunningly attractive display of seven shallow tanks in which local fish are shown as well as anemonies, starfish, lobsters and crabs. We had the privilege of watching Selby and Kathlene care for their tanks ensuring a healthy environment for their stock which is provided by local fishermen. This is the way to learn your wildlife before setting out to explore the local beaches and rock pools. The museum not only describes the fish but also the life of the fishermen and on the first floor is a typical working kitchen and a mock-up showing the family hard at work getting the bait ready for the lines. There is also an exhibit showing a yard and workshed illustrating net mending and the tows being dipped in the bark pots — a sort of home based operation similar to that which we described at Craster. There is a display showing the kippering process, the art and craft of the cooper who made the fish barrels and a simulation of the wheelhouse of a modern trawler. With its combination of holiday resort, working port, museum and the natural history extravaganza of the Farnes, Seahouses always looks busy.

In almost complete contrast Bamburgh attracts tourists but seems to absorb them without looking busy as it sucks its visitors into its many cosy little tea and coffee shops. For anyone who

Even in the 1930's regular horse drawn coach trips crossed to Holy Island from Belford.

has never seen Bamburgh two visits are essential. Firstly pick a pleasant evening and wait until dusk falls before approaching from Seahouses. The floodlit castle looks magnificent at this time and whets the appetite for a return visit to explore the settlement with its fine church and the Grace Darling Museum.

It is no wonder that Bamburgh is dominated by its castle because it was once the capital of Bernica and Northumbria. The area was first fortified by the early kings and became King Oswald's capital, but was all but wiped out by the invading Danes:–

Thy tower proud Bamburgh, mant'd they there
King Ida's castle, huge and square
From its tall rock look grimly down,
And on the swelling ocean frown,
Then from the coast they bore away,
And reached the Holy Island's bay.

Thus wrote Sir Walter Scott in _Marmion_ but as usual the search for a good plot was more important than historical accuracy.

Sir Walter looked at the Norman fortress 'huge and square' and substituted this for the Northumbrian wooden palisade set on an outcrop of the Whin Sill some 45.7 metres (150 feet) above the sea which until silting shallowed the area was almost surrounded by sea. In AD 547 Ida the Flamebearer, fierce King of Northumbria fortified the summit, called it Dinguard and from it governed the area from the Humber to the Forth. Ida's grandson Ethelfrith gave the fortress to his wife Bebba and it became known as Bebbanburgh from which the present name derives. Until England became a united Kingdom Bamburgh was a Royal town and it still gives this proud impresion today. Although the Norman's castle has now replaced the Saxon fort the well which is 45.7 metres (150 feet) deep is a tangible reminder of 8th century effort to hack down through solid basalt and then into softer but still tough sandstone.

The present castle dates from the 11th century and was stoutly built of stone to resist the Scots, but was last besieged in 1464 and was the headquarters of King Henry VI during the Wars of the Roses,when it was badly damaged by canon fire. From then on Bamburgh castle declined until it was purchased in 1704 by Lord Crewe, the influential Bishop of Durham. He restored the castle and also instituted a trust which included the setting up of a girls' boarding school within the castle, a most unusual thing to do in the days of almost total male dominance. It was stipulated that 34 small girls should be cared for until they were 16 and then they were to be found positions 'in service'. In truth these little ladies would not have been difficult to place as few girls would have had any education at all. The poor of Bamburgh were also cared for and considerable sums were devoted to the lifeboat, helping shipwrecked sailors and paying for the funerals of those drowned. With the coming of the welfare state the work of the Trust was not required and funds are now made available to retired clergy who are in need. In the late 19th century the castle was purchased by Lord Armstrong who had already spent much of his profits from his armaments and shipbuilding interests on his home at Cragside. He set about a thorough restoration, although some pedantic historians point out that it was more of a reconstruction. All we can say is that Dunstanburgh is a ruin and Bamburgh is

The majestic ruins of Lindisfarne Priory on Holy Island.

not. It is open from April to the 30 June and in September from 1 p.m. to 5 p.m. In the peak months of July and August the opening times are from 12 noon to 6 p.m. In October the castle opens from 1 p.m. to 4.30 p.m. and it closes in winter except for pre-arranged group visits. There is a shop in the old kitchens and other rooms worth spending a lot of time in are the museum, armoury, court room, the keep hall and the King's hall. The Armstrong room specialising in the man's many inventions is fascinating especially if combined with a visit to Cragside, (see chapter 6).

In Bamburgh itself, a village set around a sloping green, the chance should not be missed to visit the church and the Grace Darling Museum on Radcliffe Road. The museum is free of charge but visitors are encouraged to give a donation to the Royal National Lifeboat Institution. The delightful little shrine was opened in 1898 and on display are the heroine's clothes, schoolbooks, details of the Forfarshire wreck and obviously the little coble which Grace and her father rowed to the stricken ship. In the churchyard and fittingly overlooking the sea is an ornate memorial sited just to the north of her grave. Inside the church in St Cuthbert's chapel is another memorial which is inscribed 'To the memory of Grace Horsley Darling, a native of Bamburgh and an inhabitant of these islands.' The museum opens daily between April and September from 11 a.m. to 6 p.m. and the nearby church of St Aidan is one of the most delightful churches in Northumberland. There was a Saxon church here but nothing of this remains but the present 13th century building is one of the largest parish churches in England. It is the stained glass which should inspire the visitor in search of the history of Northumberland one of the best windows being dedicated in 1936. It shows the castles of Bamburgh and Lindisfarne to the right of which is depicted St Cuthbert surrounded by flowers, shells and of course his beloved birds. If the birds are mainly found on the Farnes the flowers are very much a feature of the extensive sand dunes which lie below the castle and sweep majestically towards Holy Island a little to the north. Here grow harebell, bird's foot trefoil and yellow rattle whilst fulmars nest in increasingly large numbers on the cliffs below Bamburgh Castle.

By far the best way to approach Holy Island otherwise known as Lindisfarne is via the attractive small town of Belford, once right on the A1, but now recently bypassed. In the days when coaches rattled along the turnpike the Bluebell Inn was a popular hostelry and it still caters well for visitors and those in search of a good restaurant meal or a substantial bar snack. We have pointed out several times in this book that one of the joys of discovering a new county is to take

The splendid Norman Arch over the gateway of Lindisfarne Priory.

home unusual presents or keepsakes. Belford provides three opportunities to do this. The Hazon Mill knitwear on the High Street is open daily from 9.30 a.m. to 4.30 p.m. except Sundays. At nearby Warenford, Norseland's Gallery sited in the Old School sells stoneware hand sculpted figurines. It is open 9 a.m. to 5 p.m. all year but stays open until 9 p.m. during the season. At Felton-le-Moor the Brent Gallery sells Lindisfarne pottery plus pictures of the countryside and wildlife. It opens daily from Easter to October from 10 a.m. to 7 p.m.

The natural history of this area is indeed rich and a real rival to the Farnes is Holy Island which can only be reached at low tide and thus careful planning is required not only to cross the causeway safely but also to ensure a safe return.

Only half the name 'Holy Island' is actually true. This lovely spot is certainly Holy but technically it is not an island but known as a tombolo which means that it is separated from the mainland only at high tide. We remember in our early school days listening to our class teacher and the vicar speak of not one Holy island, but two. We listened spellbound to the tales of Iona off Mull off the Western coast of Scotland, but even more exciting was the Northumberland Holy Island of Lindisfarne. This name derives from the Celtic 'farn' meaning land and the Lindis which was a small stream long since diverted by the forces of erosion. This once had to be crossed by pilgrims on their way to the shrine on the island. The majority of Northumbrian place names are Scandinavian based and Celtic appelations are few and far between. However long Lindisfarne has provided human sanctuary we can be sure that it has been important to wildlife for even longer and it is fitting that there is now a National Nature Reserve established here. It was this which initially attracted us to the place and we subsequently led many naturalist groups on botanising and ornithological explorations. It is, we soon found, impossible to visit Lindisfarne without it becoming immediately apparent that it is a Holy Place and our students were always fascinated by the combination of monastery, castle and wildlife. The Benedictine priory and the castle are both open but visitors' trips should be geared to the tides. These days most visitors come by private car but earlier this century regular coaches drawn by horses operated from Belford and in her book '*Northumberland*' which Ann Sitwell wrote in 1948 she noted:– 'The method of reaching Holy Island is odd but exhilarating. One telephones to Beal, a small village on the mainland opposite, for information about the tides and to order a car to take one across at the next low tide. The car is usually a battered old Ford, very much the worse for wear, and in this visitors are driven over, bumping along three miles over wet sand, following a line of posts indicating

Thousands of guillemots breed on the ledges of the Pinnacle rocks on the Farne Islands.

the safest route.' The posts are still present along the causeway but the tide times are prominently posted at both ends and emergency huts are perched on supports to save those caught out whilst walking across.

Lindisfarne's treacherous surrounding sea was appreciated by its earliest inhabitants, the Holy men who walked across to the mainland to spread the word of God. Pilgrims, perhaps converted by the Saints themselves or their followers, journeyed in the opposite direction. Two names stand out above all others — Aidan and Cuthbert. Aidan actually came from Iona and established a monastery here in AD 635 and did such good works that he was created Bishop of Lindisfarne. He died at Bamburgh but his body was brought to the wild haunting island and buried beneath the high altar of his church. Cuthbert, as we have seen, was persuaded to return from the Farnes. He was a shepherd in the Lammermuir hills who saw a vision of Aidan telling him to travel to Lindisfarne. Cuthbert was also buried at Lindisfarne and his shrine was much visited and a valuable source of income to the monks. Thus when the Viking raids of the late 7th century became intolerable the monks fled taking with them the valuable mortal remains of Cuthbert and also an illuminated copy of what is now known as the Lindisfarne Gospels and which is kept in the British Museum in London. St Cuthbert now rests at Durham and no doubt he is at peace, but we wonder if he might not rest more happily at Lindisfarne or better still close to the nest of a 'Cuddy Duck' on the Inner Farne!

In 1093 the Benedictine monks, appropriately from Durham, began a new Priory on top of the Saxon ruin and this was completed during the 12th century. The influence of the Durham architects is immediately obvious at Lindisfarne especially the so called rainbow arch with its zig-zag carving so clearly based upon the intricate work at Durham. Some of this work is on display in the Priory museum. Although fallen into ruin following the Dissolution of the monasteries in the 1540s the design of the church, also based on the Durham plan can still be seen with its nave, north and south aisles, a central apse for the high altar and a number of side altars each with its own apse. By 1613 the church had been totally stripped of its lead and exactly 300 years later the Ministry of Works set

A colony of kittiwakes.

about a restoration. The work done then was good with English Heritage now the equally thoughtful and skillfully accurate custodians. It is open from Good Friday to the end of September on a daily basis from 10 a.m. to 6 p.m. From October to Easter it opens from Tuesday to Sunday from 10 a.m. to 4 p.m.

Lindisfarne castle is of relatively recent origin built around 1550 for the defence of the realm following a survey by Sir Robert Bowes. It is a pity that most of the stone used in its construction was robbed from the disbanded priory with the buildings which were allowed to stand being used for storage. After some service during the Civil War, Fort Bebloe, as it was then called, fell into disrepair although it was still thought to have some defensive potential. Towards the end of the 19th century, however, it was abandoned, only to be bought by Edward Hudson of London with the profits of his successful magazine Country-Life. He employed Sir Edwin Lutyens to convert the castle into a gentleman's residence with arguably an unbeatable view. Gertrude Jekyll designed a small but delightful garden. Since 1944 Lindisfarne Castle has belonged to the National Trust and it is open daily except Fridays (It is open on Good Friday) to the end of September from 1 p.m. to 5.30 p.m. During October it opens Wednesday, Saturday and Sunday from 1 p.m. to 5.30 p.m.

Apart from providing the perfect example of Lutyen's best work the climb up the cobbled ramp to the portcullis gate and then to what was the original artillery position provides glorious views across the sea to the south. The Farne Islands and Bamburgh are seen at their very best from this position. To take in the magnificence of the interior design including the Ship room, a remarkably effective long gallery and a kitchen full of gleaming brass requires time and visitors should note that there are no toilet facilities in the castle. These are available in the village where there is also a rather special shop. For those in search of that special present then what about that bottle of Mead made from fermented white grapes, honey, herbs and water from the artesian well on the island. It is also fortified with spirits. During the making of a television film we enjoyed watching the production of mead and also the ever popular Lindisfarne fudge. The product is also available from a shop on the island and also at Berwick-on-Tweed described in chapter 9, but there is an extra special feeling in buying Mead so close to the abbey. The word 'herb' was of particular interest to us as we found that meadow sweet grows locally and the name is thought to derive from 'Mede-sweet'. The plant is a member of the rose family having tiny white flowers, a sweet-smell and a high concentration of salicilic acid in all parts. We know this best as aspirin. If indeed Mede-sweet was added to the brew then it is amusing to imagine it to have a built in cure for a hangover! St Aiden's winery is situated in the centre of the village just off the attractive village green. The winery has been open to the public since 1968 and each visitor is allowed a free sample of the warming liquid. In the season Lindisfarne Mead is open daily except Sunday and in winter it also closes on Saturday.

The local people are surprisingly friendly, although we could understand it if they had an ambivalent attitude to visitors. Surprisingly they do not, but it must be annoying to have hordes of people competing for space but as fishing can no longer support all the families, the tourists bring in much needed revenue. This dual function became inevitable as at Craster and Seahouses with the decline in the herring industry. Being so isolated has enabled local traditions to be maintained on Lindisfarne including a point blank refusal to refer to a pig by name. What the origin of this custom is we know not but the fisherfolk will go to any lengths not to use the word and substitute 'articles', 'grumfits' or even 'yon things'. One still has to be careful when tucking into bacon and eggs at one of the many cosy little cottages offering bed and breakfast not to mention the word pig. There is another custom observed at each wedding where to ensure a happy life the bride has to jump over the 'petting stool' situated at the east end of the churchyard.

The parish church of St Mary the Virgin is 12th century but this almost certainly replaced an earlier Saxon structure dedicated to who else but St Cuthbert. In the chancel wall there is plenty of evidence of Saxon stonework, the north aisle is a fine example of the late Norman style probably around 1150 whilst the chancel, which is very plain, is 13th century and a south aisle a century later. There are on display copies of both the Lindisfarne Gospels and the Book of Kells. A page of the Gospels have been beautifully embroidered by the women of the parish and in 1970 it was laid around the high altar.

Nobody can visit Lindisfarne without feeling the peace of the place, but if at all possible an overnight stay should be made in order to experience being cut off and allow Holy Island to complete its halo of magic. Time can then be taken to follow the walk around the island which is 3½ miles (6 km) long and around 1 mile (1.5 km) at its widest point. The walk will bring into view the beacon obelisks built in 1860 and maintained by Trinity House. Their original function was to guide ships into the harbour which brought coal and lime. The disused limekilns similar to those at Beadnell and Seahouses can be seen on the shore below the castle. In the summer season dune plants grow in profusion including bird's foot trefoil and yellow rattle whilst in winter the birdwatching is often spectacular as wildfowl and waders seek shelter from the pounding sea. We have watched brent geese, Bewick swans and several species of duck including common and velvet scoter, red breasted merganser, wigeon, goldeneye and of course hundreds of eider. Waders include sanderling, turnstone, dunlin, knot, bar tailed godwit whilst on spring passage we have seen greenshank and on one occasion a whimbrel. Lindisfarne is a naturalist's paradise and Holy Island is heaven to the historian.

Between Holy Island and Bamburgh is the quiet Budle Bay, now the haunt for thousands of birds, but all has not always been so deserted. In 1247 Henry III founded the Borough of Warrenmouth here intending it to serve Bamburgh and be a serious rival to Newcastle. Nothing now remains of this enterprise but the site is thought to be that now occupied by Heather Cottages. The settlement was later called Newtown but in 1621 this was described as 'desolate'.

From Holy Island to Berwick-upon-Tweed is a short but pleasant drive along the A1 but two diversions should be made to visit chapelries established on the mainland by the Benedictine monks of Lindisfarne in the 12th century. These are at Ancroft and Lowick. Two more were established at Kyloe and Tweedmouth. Ancroft is the only one of the four to have preserved most of its Norman stonework and its huge square tower was once used as a pele tower. This combination of church and pele is most unusual. The prior of St Anne's was also expected to deal with the spiritual needs of St Bartholomew church at Tweedmouth. There was a church at Tweedmouth from Saxon times but this was destroyed by Danish raiders around AD 870. A second church was erected around 1145 but it was replaced in 1783 and restored in 1903.

Lowick church is dedicated to St John the Baptist, the present building being erected as a replacement for a Norman church. Lowick lies on the old Roman road running south from Tweedmouth. The Tweed is a true boundary river and an ideal place to explore the northern boundary of Northumberland.

CHAPTER 9

Around Berwick-Upon-Tweed

For a town which has spent part of its life in Scotland and part in England it would be reasonable for Berwick to have developed a split personality. It even plays its football in the Scottish league and yet the town has more English and Newcastle supporters than many towns further south. Berwick-upon-Tweed however, never had problems with its identity — it is quite simply a well fortified border town. These days it even lives at peace with its tourists which are discovering the area in ever increasing numbers. There are excellent car parks, a large Information Centre open in the summer and has two market days — Wednesday and Saturday. Early closing is Thursday.

Long before we ever thought of writing about our discoveries, family holidays were spent around Berwick, usually in a caravan near Spittal on the south bank of the Tweed. We watched terns diving into the sea, salmon fishermen plying their trade using methods developed over many centuries; we have watched facilities for tourists develop over the years, bought provisions in and around the colourful open air market and taken home supplies of a mint flavoured sweet called the Berwick Cockle made by William Cowe and Sons on Bridge Street. On Main Street in Spittal we have visited the Berwick Salmon Fisheries Company and bought supplies of smoked salmon to take home. Actually none ever actually arrived as we know nothing better than smoked salmon and a bottle of chablis eaten in a caravan! We have lost count of the number of times we have explored Berwick town, but always feel the need to return as we have never ever failed to find something new, even about its history. And then there are the mute swans which have long been a feature of the river especially beneath and around the bridges. The Tweed is one of the finest salmon rivers in Britain and is spanned by three splendid bridges and arguably the finest is the 28 span Royal Border bridge designed by Robert Stephenson to carry the important rail-link into the town lying on the London-Edinburgh route. Just as at

Berwick market is popular with residents and tourists alike.

Newcastle the planners almost destroyed a magnificent castle to accommodate the station, built in 1850. The Great Hall is now a waiting room. It is too late to cry over spilled milk but what a shame that the history of the castle is only told by a plaque above the platform telling the traveller that here once stood the Great Hall of the Castle in which Edward 1st of England, the Hammer of the Scots, announced that he would support the claim of John Balliol as King of Scotland and thus triggered 300 years of war between the two fiercely proud countries. There are still other remnants of the castle including the wall running down to the Tweed from the 16th century water tower. Henry was certainly trespassing because Berwick stood on the north bank of the river which was the obvious border between England's Tweedmouth and Scotland's Berwick. Such a strategically important place was bound to be the subject of conflict. Originally one of Scotland's most important ports, Berwick changed hands 14 times until it finally became English in 1428. Even then it was given special status to keep the Scots happy and was accepted as a free borough, and in acts of Parliament Berwick was given a mention on its own. It is on record that Berwick-upon-Tweed is still at war with Russia. In 1854 it was listed as joining in the hostilities but Berwick was omitted from the 1856 peace treaty! Fortunately the Russians do not take the threat seriously and the town's Elizabethan walls are not needed as protection but as a promenade for tourists and residents alike. Actually there are two sets of walls, the first circuit being built during the reign of Edward II (1307–27) but little remains of these. The outer ring of defence is, however, complete and Berwick is thus the most completely defended town in Britain. This was started in the reign of Mary Tudor and completed during the great Elizabethan age. They are of the Italian design, built to allow the maximum use of well positioned artillery, and the only example of this arrangement now to be found in Britain. Three of the projecting bastions still remain and are shaped like flat arrowheads. Only one of the original gates, Cowport, remains and close to this a flight of steps leads up onto the ramparts made of huge heaps of earth. The circular walk around the walls takes about an hour to complete, but at least three should be allowed giving time to picnic or sit on one of the many seats and look out over the flat lands and beyond them the sea. In between looking at the canon in the Cumberland Bastion and exploring the church and the Barracks we once picnicked on yet more Tweed salmon followed by a generous helping of fresh black cherries. The view into the town from the walls allows easy access to the church and the barracks both of which have a fascinating and almost unique history.

Berwick-upon-Tweed barracks developed from the town's military tradition, as from the reign of Edward 1st this has been a soldiers' town. As the men had to be billeted with civilians, this often led to friction and it was only a matter of time before a purpose built barracks was constructed. Work began on a building designed by Vanburgh in the early 18th century and was completed by 1721. As usual bureaucracy moves in mysterious ways and it was some time after the completion before the troops could move in. There was apparently no money left to pay for furniture and utensils. The citizens of Berwick soon raised the funds in order to be rid of their guests! The Barracks are now open from Good Friday or 1 April depending which is earlier to 30 September from

10 a.m. to 6 p.m. The out of season opening is from 10 a.m. to 4 p.m. Tuesday to Sunday. The barracks have changed little since they were first constructed and on display is an exhibition called 'By Beat of Drum' which traces the history of the British Infantryman between 1660 and 1880. It includes two accurately reconstructed rooms, one laid out as a barrack room, and the other as an army schoolroom. Very few recruits were able to read or write and the army, then as now, believed that educated men can more easily follow instructions. From 1881 the barracks was the headquarters of the King's Own Scottish Borderers and their regimental museum is housed in the East Block of the barracks. In the Clock Block is the Borough Museum and Art Gallery. This is open daily except Sunday and Monday in winter. It houses the Burrell Collection of fine art and also good displays of local history, archaeology and natural history which is very impressive hereabouts. Some of the art collection is also of great interest and includes French impressionist paintings with some fine examples of the work of Degas, 18th century glassware from Venice, German pewter, Ming vases, Medieval brass, and Japanese Imari pottery, all of which are permanent. There are also temporary exhibitions arranged several times each year and lectures and children's activities are also regularly organised.

Near the barracks is the unusual parish church of the Holy Trinity. During the Civil War of the 1640s Berwick was occupied by large numbers of Parliamentary Troops who were very religious, either because they wanted to be or because they were forced to be; in any event the parish church was too small and probably too Catholic for their Puritan taste. A new church was built, one of only two constructed in the Commonwealth period, and it had neither spire, stained glass nor bells. The other is Staunton Harold in Lincolnshire. This led to confusion as the faithful were summoned to prayer by the bells in the soaring steeple of the Guildhall which from a distance looks surprisingly church-like. Its 150 feet (45.7 metres) high steeple still dominates Marygate and the market place. Each evening the curfew bell is rung at 8 p.m., a reminder of its medieval function, and Berwick-upon-Tweed still holds an annual Riding of the Bounds ceremony on the 1st of May, a most colourful ceremony.

The old town walls at Berwick-upon-Tweed.

The classically designed Guildhall once served as a jail, the prisoners being kept in the upper storey and exercised on the balcony set around the roof. The lower storey was once the colonaded buttermarket and has now been restored and houses a coffee bar and shop. Liquid of a stronger nature may be found on the Palace Green.

Lindisfarne Limited is a museum displaying artefacts from the wine and spirit industry. The house overlooking the yard was the Governor's house which was contemporary with the Barracks. The yard itself was originally orchards and once the home of the Borders Brewery. Lindisfarne Limited bought the yard in 1974 and have been gradually restoring it ever since. It is open from Monday to Saturday from 9 a.m. to 5 p.m. Monday to Saturday inclusive from Easter to September. Out of season it only opens from Monday to Friday. The wine and spirit museum has on display a set of coopers' tools and an original Victorian chemist's shop has been recreated. After the drinks industry was metricated in 1980 most equipment became obsolete and how nostalgic it was to take a step back into history to see some of this equipment. An even longer journey backwards in time is the display of windows from the first-class lounge of the SS *Olympic* the sister ship of the *Titanic*. We have already seen other artefacts from this ship at the Swan Hotel in Alnwick. Entry to Lindisfarne Limited is free, and a visit to the pot shop and perfumery based in the old stables and opened in 1989 will be irresistible to those in search of an unusual present. We can never resist buying a couple of bottles of Lindisfarne mead, and tasting sessions do much to boost sales. There is free parking and a very pleasant picnic site.

Whatever new attractions may be developed Berwick's attraction for tourists will always be its Elizabethan walls and the three magnificent bridges which link it to Tweedmouth. The Old Bridge dates to 1624 and has 15 elegant arches spanning a distance of 1,137 feet (346.4 metres). It is constructed of fine red sandstone and its construction is said to have been suggested by James VI of Scotland whilst on his way to become James I of England and unite the two countries. The dual monarch is said to have been apprehensive at crossing the rickety old wooden bridge situated just upstream from the present span. 'Is there ne'er a man in Berwick who can work stanes to mak' a brig ower the Tweed'. Whether this is true or apocryphal is debatable, but Berwick did have the architect and the masons required and the fine old bridge bears witness to their skill. The Royal Border Bridge shows that these early skills were still present between 1847 and 1850 when George Stephenson's design was implemented by 2,000 workmen at a cost of £253,000. The magnificent viaduct towers 126 feet (38.3 metres) above the Tweed, is supported by 28 arches and is 728 yards (665.3 metres) long. It has been calculated that 1,710,000 bricks went into the construction of the bridge. The rather uninspiring Royal Tweed Bridge was built in 1928 and took the pressure of heavy traffic off the Old Bridge and in the late 1980s the A1 bypass has reduced through traffic to such an extent that it is now a pleasure to drive into Berwick and there are few hold ups in what was once a notorious bottleneck. The Royal Tweed Bridge does, however, have some claim to fame as its northern span measures 371 feet (113.03 metres) and is the longest single concrete span in Britain.

It is seldom realised by first time visitors that Berwick and Tweedmouth were both important ports set on the estuary of the river. Berwick harbour was probably used around AD 518 when it was part of the Kingdom of Bernicia founded by Ida and there are written records of its dealings in the 9th century with King Malcolm II of Scotland claiming the north bank of the Tweed in 1018, and this tension was not relaxed until the union of 1603. Obviously this led to numerous skirmishings and several pitched battles including the bloody affair at Flodden described later, but the battle of Halidon Hill fought in 1333 was a fierce encounter much closer to Berwick. The location is still easy to recognise and from it there are magnificent views over the town. This battle, however, was caused not so much because of the enmity between the English and the old enemy but because of Scot's politics. In 1314 Robert Bruce had given the English a fearsome beating at Bannockburn but following his death in 1329 he was succeeded by his son David II who was only seven years old. This led to a power struggle with five regents in four years each usurped in turn by force of arms. The third regent was Balliol and he actually laid claim to the throne before being overthrown and chased over the border into England. Edward III of England supported his claim and laid siege to Berwick both by land and by means of a sea blockade. This led to the 14th century equivalent of a phoney war in which the Scots agreed to surrender after a period of time, hoping that a relieving force would arrive. They gave hostages to Balliol as a sign of good faith. The Scots sent to effect the raising of the siege realised that the task was all but impossible and tried to draw away the English army by butchery and pillaging villages to the south of Berwick. Edward III was not to be deterred, kept his position and hanged some hostages including two sons of the governor. A battle was now inevitable and after some manoeuvring the smaller English force secured the top of the hill overlooking the boggy terrain beneath. Used effectively for the first time the English long bow destroyed the Scots without much hand-to-hand fighting being necessary. Subsequent battles in the 14th and 15th century involved manoeuvres to give the archers an advantage with the same tactics of war still being applied, but these days the artillery and tanks are involved.

Tweedmouth, on the English side of the old border, is now overshadowed by Berwick but the views from it across the Tweed are truly spectacular. In mid July a ceremony is held here which dates back to 1292 and celebrates the fact that here one of the best salmon rivers in Britain reaches the sea. The local schools hold a ballot to elect a 'Salmon Queen' and her crowning heralds the start of Feast week, centred around a church service but involves lots of fun and a traditional salmon supper. It is at this time and from this angle that the estuary can be seen for what it has always been — a busy harbour around which have grown settlements looking inland and up river. Berwick is the commercial and shopping centre but Tweedmouth and Spittal have the beaches and cater for holidaymakers as opposed to visitors. At one time a feature of the whole area was a number of ice houses which were used to keep the fish fresh. The ice was collected in winter and the houses had deep cool cellars which prevented it from melting. With the coming of the fast railway link these became redundant. The railway also brought increasing numbers of visitors and Berwick entered upon its new role of a tourist centre and this is an increasing source of revenue for the town and the area. The number of places of interest is large and varied but among our favourites are the Union Chain Bridge near Horncliffe, Norham, Tillmouth, Cornhill, Wark-on-Tweed, Carham plus Ford and Etal villages and the site of Flodden field above the hamlet of Branxton.

Some seven miles upstream from Berwick and connecting England with Scotland is one of the oldest suspension bridges and situated close to the village of Horncliffe. The Union Suspension bridge by its very name indicates its border import-ance a fact symbolised by roses emblazoned at one end and thistles at the other. The motto *vis unita fortior* — meaning 'stronger in unity' probably meant more in 1820 than is the case today when time has healed most, if not all, of the old wounds. The bridge, designed by the naval officer Captain Samuel Brown, was the first suspension bridge able to take vehicular traffic and Telford studied the union in great detail whilst planning the Menai suspension bridge. Its dimensions are, to say the least, impressive having a length of 437 feet (133 metres) and a width of 18 feet (5.5 metres). On the English side of the bridge is a honey farm run by Willie Robson with whom we once made a television film. We were astounded at his control of his bees which he regards as his friends and also with

The railway bridge at Berwick-upon-Tweed.

the hand and face cream which he makes from bee products. These act as a cross between a cosmetic and an ointment. The farm is not regularly open to the public, but groups are made very welcome.

Just beyond the bridge is yet another historic and attractive village named Norham and meaning North-Ham because it was the most northerly possession of the Bishops of Durham. These clerics not only handled the spiritual needs of the area, but were also like feudal war lords being responsible for the defence of the English borders against the Scots.

> Day set on Norham's castle steep,
> And Tweed's fair river broad and deep
> And Cheviot's mountain lone:
> The battled towers, the donjon keep
> The loop-holed wall whose captives weep
> In Yellow lustre shone.

Thus wrote Sir Walter Scott in *Marmion* in which he describes the build up to the battle of Flodden, with the Scots causing much damage to Norham castle. Now maintained by English

Heritage the castle is open from Good Friday or 1 April (whichever is earlier) to 30 September between 10 a.m. and 6 p.m. From October to March it is open from Tuesday to Sunday between 10 a.m. to 4 p.m. The castle is beautifully set on a grassy mound overlooking the River Tweed and was built in the 12th century to control the crossing which it did until Flodden when it was battered by the huge canon Mons Meg which is now at Edinburgh Castle. The Norman keep still gives a feeling of strength and the inner moat is also very evident, but other main buildings are now seen only in outline. The church also retains much of its Norman structure, built in 1165 and dedicated to St Cuthbert. Although there have been renovations since the time the Prince Bishops established the church, the chancel, the south arcade and several pillars on the north side are clearly Norman. The church was often used as a rendezvous between Scots and English politicians and it was here or in the Great Hall of the castle that Edward 1st considered which King he would support north of the border. The church holds a very special event each year at midnight on 13 February. This is the time when the vicar and the local fishermen meet to have their nets blessed to mark the beginning of the still lucrative salmon industry. The service is conducted by lantern light and is said to relive the miracle where Christ caused a shoal of fish to swim into his disciples' nets and which is described in St John's gospel.

Just outside the village now consisting mainly of plain but attractive stone cottages is Norham station, with the old station house now an attractive museum. Norham was on the Kelso Branch line which was the oldest in Northumberland but was closed in 1965. It opens during the Easter weekend between 1.30 and 5.30 p.m. and then opens again from May to October between Monday and Thursday from 1.30 p.m. and 5.30 p.m. but it is open on every Bank Holiday. The museum includes the original signal box, booking office and porter's room. It is a pity that a section of this border route was not kept open but it is now too late as the track has been lifted. It would be an ideal place for a brief encounter because Norham even brought romance into the life of the austere Scots religious reformer John Knox. It was here in 1549 that he first met Margaret Bowes whose father was governor of the castle. The history

Berwick-on-Tweed harbour photographed in the 1930's by Reece Winstone.

of Norham did not begin just in Norman times being known as Ubbanford prior to this period. There was a church here dedicated to St Coelwulph who was King of Northumberland and who was brought to Ubbanford for burial. The church was dedicated in AD 830. The valley of the River Tweed has thus been an important area for many centuries.

One of the major tributaries of the Tweed is the delightful little Till with the two merging at the village of Tillmouth. Twizel Bridge, dating from the 15th century and funded by a female member of the locally influential Selby family still stands its 90 foot (27.4 metres) span adding extra beauty to the Till. It is quite a narrow bridge soaring gracefully to a single arch 40 feet above the river and across which the Earl of Surrey marched a column of soldiers in an effort to deceive the Scot's King James IV on his way to Flodden. The English manoeuvres may well have contributed to the resounding English victory. Overlooking the river is the ruin of Twizzel Castle which was never part of the border history being the idea of Sir Francis Blake in 1770 but never actually completed. There is some good walking hereabouts and a well signed footpath leads through a splendidly varied woodland and in just over one mile the confluence of the Till and the Tweed is reached. On the opposite bank is a now sadly ruined chapel one of the many places where the monks from Lindisfarne halted as they carried the body of St. Cuthbert to prevent it falling into the hands of the piratical Norsemen. Those who wonder why a pile of bones was important should remember that pilgrims who came to pay homage to the Saints often contributed large sums to the monastery coffers. Another span has been built near Twizel Bridge and carries the A698 to Cornhill, Wark-on-Tweed and Carham.

Cornhill-on-Tweed controls the south or English end of the Coldstream Bridge for centuries one of the main crossing points of the Tweed. Although Cornhill is pretty in its own right it is dominated by the Scots market town of Coldstream famous for providing the origins of one of the finest guard's regiments of the British Army. Actually to say that the regiment originated here is not quite correct. General Monk formed the unit in 1650 from Fenwick's and Heselrige's Regiments with the intention of fighting Scottish Presbyterians. In 1658 the HQ was sited at Coldstream and after a period of supporting the Commonwealth, General Monk and his guards were largely instrumental in restoring Charles II to the throne in 1660. In the market square the old Guard's House is now a museum. The linking bridge was built by John Smeaton between 1763 and 1766. When Robert Burns travelled he kept a diary and from Coldstream he crossed into England over the 'glorious River Tweed, clear, majestic, Fine Bridge.' Yes indeed a fine bridge over a lovely river and upstream of Cornhill is another historic village at Wark-on-Tweed.

These days Wark appears to be an unimportant hamlet but in its day the castle was one of the most strategically valuable. It was constructed in the 12th century and was continually under threat as the border wars raged; it was knocked down and rebuilt many times. It was here in 1305 that the Order of the Garter is said to have originated, an event described in chapter seven. Wark took a fearsome beating as the Scots prepared for Flodden and following the union of 1603 fell into such a decline that all which remains today is a mound of earth or motte standing forlornly in a field close to the road. Beyond Wark on the B6350 is the now almost remote village of Carham, but it too has seen more than its share of fierce border history. The

Redden Burn has since 1222 been the border between England and Scotland and thus the perfect place for the wardens of the two sides to meet and do their best to keep some semblance of law; not so much as protection against armies but against the fortune seeking border reivers who were at their most active during the 15th and 16th centuries. There is history a plenty in this area and none is better preserved than that at Ford, Etal and Flodden.

Like strawberries and cream Ford and Etal are best enjoyed as a pair. Here on the borders of England and Scotland, an area of very low population, is one of Britain's tourist traps which provide more than just a feel of more gentle Cotswold countryside — there is even thatch in evidence. A visit to these heavenly twins, situated 9 miles south west of Berwick between Wooler and Coldstream, should never be rushed, for nowhere in the county are there so many tourist attractions within such a small or more attractive area.

We arrived in Etal on a gentle early summer evening with the warm sun reflecting from the stonework of the ruined castle, maintained by English Heritage, but freely open at all times and from which a footpath leads down to the ford over River Till. A guide to the castle can be purchased at the Post Office. In 1250 the Manor of Etal was in the hands of the Manners family who had a dwelling on what was described as a previously occupied site. In the 1340s during the reign of Edward III Robert Manners obtained what was known as a licence to crenellate. This was necessary to prevent ambitious landowners having castles substantial enough to threaten the Crown. Only those who would be trusted were granted a licence but the Manner's case was very obviously a strong one since they were so close to the border that the Scots had to be resisted. The first part to be built was the substantial keep with the gatehouse and curtain walls constructed later. The Manner's family left the castle in 1547 and the union of England with Scotland under James VI of the latter and first of the former, meant the threat of cross border conflict has gone. The castle therefore settled down to centuries of inactivity, and as an unofficial quarry but since 1976 the English Heritage have demonstrated its expertise on the restoration.

The tomb of Sir Ralph de Grey and his wife in St. Peter's church at Chillingham is one of the finest to be found anywhere in Britain.

In the village itself is the Black Bull which is the only thatched inn in the whole of Northumberland. For those who enjoy taking home a traditional gift from a holiday then a visit to the Errol Hut Smithy at Leatham Hill should be high on the discoverer's list. Here craftsmen in wood and metal produce both useful and decorative implements. There is also an antique traction caravan, in which there is sometimes another craft on display. A lady spins on a locally made wheel and the musical clack of this instrument blends beautifully with the sound of wood being planed and metal being hammered.

At the opposite end of the village is Etal Manor the home built for the Joicey family whose estates also include the village of Ford. Although the manor is not open to the public the grounds which are a riot of colour are on occasional Sundays open. At the backend of the year the gardens are famous for a dazzling display of autumn crocus.

Within easy range of Etal is Duddo, a tiny hamlet close to which are the Duddo Stones, one of Northumberland's most important ancient monuments. There are only five stones between 5 and 10 feet (2–3 metres) high are all that remains of a once substantial stone circle. Just as at Stonehenge there is and has been for a long time often heated discussions regarding the meaning of the stones. We can certainly discount the Druid Temple idea said to be associated with human sacrifice: much more reasonable is the suggestion the stones were set at precise mathematical angles and served as astronomical observatories. Duddo has been dated to around 2,000 BC. We who have clocks and central heating are largely independent of the seasons, do not realise how important a knowledge of astronomical events were to these ancient civilisations. The stone circle can only be reached from the village on foot, but what a delightful walk it is to reach the circle the stones often being used as a perch by skylarks, meadow pipit and especially by the summer visiting wheatears reorganised by the prominent white rump. Judging by the number of artefacts found around the circle there must have been a substantial Bronze Age settlement in the area. A more recent memorial is Duddo castle destroyed by the Scots before Flodden but restored on the orders of Elizabeth 1st. It is now, alas a ruin.

If Etal was the focus of an ancient civilisation then Ford is an equally fine example of a model village, the dream of Louisa, the Marchioness of Waterford who was so highly thought of in the Royal circle that she was one of the bridesmaids at the wedding of Queen Victoria and Prince Albert. Louisa was a remarkably good artist and had she needed to support herself she could easily have done so. She built the village school, now known as the Lady Waterford Hall, and decorated its walls with splendid murals. The good lady certainly took her time and the murals are a record of the local inhabitants over a period of around 20 years. Although the themes were religious she used the villagers as her models and many visitors still return to Ford to view their ancestors. Louisa also spent some time restoring her family home and Ford Castle, which is not open to the public, but was saved as a result of her efforts. It is let to the Northumberland Education Committee by the local landowner Lord Joicey. Built in 1282 the castle was strengthened during the 14th century by Sir William Heron who was the High Sheriff of Northumberland. It was badly damaged by the Scots on their way to the battle of Flodden and only two of the original four towers remain. It was substantially restored in 1761 by Sir John Deleval and then by Lady Waterford who is buried in the 13th century church which is close to the castle. Although the church was altered during Lady Waterford's regime the substantial bell tower may well be original. Although the castle serves another use the kitchen gardens can be visited as they are the site of Northumbria Nurseries. It specialises in hardy ornamental plants which thrive in this tough country on the fringe of the Cheviot mountain range.

There is plenty of accommodation for visitors, especially those who enjoy good bed and breakfast establishments and there is certainly plenty to see including Heatherslaw Light railway, the Heatherslaw Corn Mill, the Old Power House; whilst for those who enjoy exploring from horseback Kimmerston Riding Centre is an ideal base. The Heatherslaw Light Railway is a 15 inch gauge track running between Etal and Heatherslaw following the valley of the River Till. A regular service is operated between Easter and the end of October from 10 a.m. to 5 p.m. Heatherslaw is situated between Etal and Ford and there is much to see in the hamlet itself including the John Sinclair Railway museum which specialises in items from the old North Eastern railway. It is open at the same time as the Light Railway and entry is by donation. Close to the station is the restored 19th century Heatherslaw Corn Mill driven by an undershot waterwheel. The sound and sight of corn being milled is a lasting memory and most visitors return home with a bag of

The cross at Flodden Field marks the site of one of the most famous battles ever fought in Britain.

flour or an item purchased from the craft shop. The Granary Cafe is an integral part of the mill and specialises in home made teas, although the lunches are also of high quality. The mill complex is open between Easter and the end of October from 10 a.m. to 6 p.m. with the cafe closing at 5.30 p.m. The Old Power House also overlooking the River Till has been converted into a workshop specialising in modern and reproduction furniture and is open on weekdays from 8.30 a.m. to 5 p.m. and also on weekends during the tourist season. Kimmerston Riding Centre is only a mile outside Ford and lessons are given to beginners and there are recognised tracks up into the Cheviot Hills and also down to the coast. Many visitors who enjoy the open-air and like to have their dog with them make use of the facilities offered by Kimmerston County Holidays who have several self catering holidays on offer. These and the riding centre operate throughout the year. Good bar snacks are available at the well named Friendly Hound Inn situated at Ford Common.

From this area it is easy to reach the site of the battle of Flodden Field near the hamlet of Branxton. The night prior to the battle James IV of Scotland spent at Ford Castle. By the afternoon of September 9 1513 the King's body was lying in the chancel of St Paul's church at Branxton.

James IV who became King of Scotland in 1488 was a popular monarch who had restored the self respect of the nation, stabilised its currency, improved the judicial system and paid great attention to the development of commerce. In addition he made a sensible marriage and promised peace with England but unfortunately these proved too difficult to sustain and led to failure. In 1502 the King married Margaret Tudor the daughter of Henry VII, both monarchs no doubt hoping to avoid costly border skirmishes and allowing their energies to be devoted to their ailing and weakened Kingdoms. In 1512, however, James made a fatal error by renewing an 'auld alliance' with Louis XII of France. As his brother-in-law Henry VIII was about to invade France in support of the Holy League this put James in a no-win situation. James tried to negotiate to prevent Henry going on with this venture and even sent an envoy to the English camp in Flanders but they failed to change his mind. James IV was a man of honour and he and Henry were thus on a collision course and a decisive battle was inevitable. James arrived at

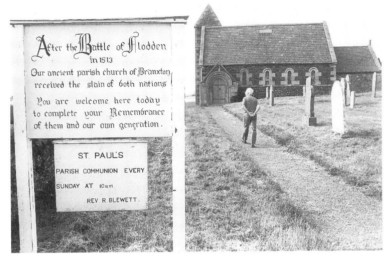

After the **Battle** of **Flodden** in 1513

Our ancient parish church of Branxton received the slain of both nations

You are welcome here today to complete your Remembrance of them and our own generation.

ST. PAUL'S

PARISH COMMUNION EVERY

SUNDAY AT 10am

REV. R. BLEWETT

Here at St. Paul's church lie the remains of those slaughtered at Flodden.

Flodden full of confidence after having inflicted losses on the English at Wark, Norham, Etal and Ford. Perhaps these victories instilled in him some over-confidence because he was definitely out-manoeuvred by the Earl of Surrey. Despite facing a force of 30,000 the English secured the best ground and almost 10,000 Scots including the King were killed and the rest were put to flight. Few battlefields have such a feel as Flodden, the summit of the 509 feet (155 metres) hill graced by a cross erected early this century. Below this is a discreetly screened car park from which steps lead up through a field of barley to the cross. Here is a board protected from the weather which explains the background to the battle, the disposition of the troops and the evolution and conclusion of one of the bloodiest battles ever fought on British soil. Little has changed since that fateful day and the ditches in which so many men perished — even the victorious English had 5,000 men killed — are still apparent. St Paul's church where many are buried lies snugly below, a notice board at its entrance asking visitors to think of those young men who fell. Despite the centuries which have passed Flodden has the distinct feel of a First World War battlefield in Flanders. Here in 1513 Henry VIII and James IV failed to find ground for compromise. Branxton is nothing more than a peaceful hamlet overlooked by Flodden and Branxton Hills, both of which are the same height. The church of St Paul was extensively restored in 1849 but the architect had the sense to preserve the chancel arch the last memorial to a very formidable monarch. A more recent memorial is what is known as the cement menagerie a collection of animals displayed in a nearby cottage garden.

The journey by car from Flodden to Berwick-on-Tweed is quick and attractive, but the conveyance of the body of James IV was an altogether sadder affair. One final area to visit whilst discovering the area within reach of Berwick is around Chillingham, home of the most fascinating herds of cattle to be found anywhere in the world. Chillingham can, however, be just as easily explored by using Wooler as a base. The town rightly describes itself as the gateway to the Cheviot and although it looks rather plain there are plenty of good cafes and several excellent shops. As it is set on a breezy slope Wooler at one time had an ambition to become a health resort and Grace Darling visited the town in an unsuccessful attempt to cure her terminal consumption. Wooler is close to the Northumberland National Park and during the summer there is a portable Tourist Information Centre providing a comprehensive overview of the area. The name derives from the old Norse word Woolan which means a place for cattle and it may well have been a vital drove road at the junction of several streams running down from the Cheviots. The hills provided many hiding places for the Reivers and Wooler, as a frontier town, must have resembled the wild west at its most dangerous. The town must have demanded a protective castle but alas little of the Norman structure remains and only the steep mound on which it stood can be detected. Wooler appears to be mainly a Victorian town but this is because two disastrous fires in 1772 and 1862 destroyed many of the older buildings, but the atmosphere has been retained by the continued presence of cattle and sheep markets, a reminder when its livestock fairs were famous. Probably the most famous sons of Wooler were the Dalziel brothers George, Edward, John and Thomas who were all skillful wood engravers. In Victorian

Etal Castle and Gatehouse above the banks of the River Till.

times they provided the illustrations for many books and also worked on the early editions of *Punch* magazine. In recent times Wooler has become a popular resort for anglers and walkers especially those who stroll with a purpose. The natural history hereabouts is impressive, but it is for the wealth of archeological sites that the land between Wooler and the Cheviots are famous. Some of these walks are described in the many leaflets on sale at the Information Centre. One of our favourite strolls leads to Kettle's Camp a prehistoric fort close to which is an old wishing well. By following the Colegate Burn the well named Happy Valley is reached and the walk provides ample opportunity for observing dipper, grey wagtail all the year round plus the exciting and active common sandpiper in the spring. Just to the south west of Wooler is the Harthope Valley with excellent walks along another crystal stream, the Harthope Burn. In the summer Wooler holds a week long carnival and the Glendale show attracts large crowds. It is the Cheviots, however, which attract the visitors but even so this range of hills is the least explored of all the hilly areas of Britain. The fact that the Ministry of Defence owns and protects some of the area should not deter the walker. It should not be forgotten that this is a tough mountainous area. The Cheviot was itself some 300 million years ago an active volcano and is 2676 feet (816 metres) in height. The crater is still obvious as are the lava flows which rolled down during the last eruption. Other substantial peaks include the cone shaped Hedgechife Hill at 2348 feet (715 metres) and Combe Fell which is 2132 feet (650 metres). From Wooler the best route to the Cheviot is to follow Cheviot Street on which stands the Anchor Inn and off towards Earle passing the Pin Well en route. It was here that travellers once dropped pins on May day which was said to guarantee good luck over the following year. There is a small museum at Earle Hill which is open during the summer and which has on display farm and household antiquitie including ploughs, tools, needlework, toys and a good collection of old photographs. Beyond Earle is a riverside picnic area at Middleton Hall and Happy Valley is also not far away. Further upstream along the Harthope Burn is Langleeford, well known to Sir Walter Scott and also to those climbing the Cheviot, the village being an ideal starting point for the walk to the summit.

Wooler is also an ideal base for those who prefer to explore by car. One lovely route follows the B6348 to Chatton, Chillingham, Hepburn Wood, Ross Castle and Hedgeley Moor and onto Ingram; we have driven this route several times and in all weathers and have parked in most of its laybys to explore something new which delights each separate visit. Nobody en route to the fascinating castle at Chillingham should drive through Chatton without stopping and doing some exploring on foot. Close to the village are thirteen ancient camps and enclosures, all marked on the O.S. map but not always easy to find. The perseverance is, however, well worth the effort for here is the earliest history of England's most northerly county. Take a look also at the church and the vicarage which incoporates yet another medieval pele tower. The parish church of the Holy Cross was built to provide tithes for the monks of Alnwick Abbey between 1157 and 1184 on ground provided by William de Vesey. When the abbeys were dissolved in the late 1530s Chatton was given to the Percys. The Norman church was burned down in 1713 and the present church built close by but not actually on the original site. The organ is of particular interest having come from Magdalen College, Oxford for whom it was built by Holdich of London. Just off the road between Chatton and Lowick another religious site is signposted — St Cuthbert's cave where 'Cuddy' is said to have lived for a time as a hermit.

Only about two miles from Chatton is Chillingham which also has a remarkably fine church dedicated to St Peter. Despite an extensive restoration in 1967 much ancient stonework remains as well as some attractive 19th century box pews. The joy, however, is the 15th century tomb of Sir Ralph de Grey which well deserves to be famous. The owner of Chillingham and his wife Elizabeth are commemorated in the huge carved tomb which at one time seems to have been brightly painted and some trace of the original colouring can still be seen. Chillingham was once the home of the Tankervilles and in 1344 Sir Thomas de Heban obtained permission to crenellate the castle and which later passed into the hands of the Grey family of Wark-on-Tweed and then onto the Bennets by marriage. This restored the original family as Bennet was the name of the Earls of Tankerville. The castle is beautifully sited overlooking the River Till and after centuries of ruin and neglect it was deserted in 1933. Had it not been for Sir Humphrey Wakefield who bought the castle probably because his wife was related to the Grey family, Chillingham would have crumbled to dust. The castle has now been restored to reveal a medieval family fortress with a jousting course, a rather horrendous dungeon and an even more alarming torture chamber. There are also antique furnishings, paintings, tapestries and a varied selection of armour. The gardens have also been restored and the whole is open from May to September from 1.30 p.m. to 5.30 p.m. It closes on Tuesdays and no dogs are allowed. There is a souvenir and an antique shop plus a rather pleasant restaurant which specialises in home-baked teas. In late September there is a music festival which has a rapidly growing reputation. The castle can be visited at any time by groups who can book fishing, clay pigeon shooting, and a good meal. Thus Chillingham is now a fitting focus for those who wish to see one of the world's most interesting breeds of cattle.

Chillingham white cattle are the direct descendants of the wild cattle which once roamed the forests of Britain. They

Here at Chainbridge is one of the earliest examples of a suspension bridge, and which was used as a model for the Clifton bridge across the Avon at Bristol.

are unique in the sense that they have never been crossed with any domestic breed. For the past 700 years they have been enclosed in Chillingham Park. The park can be visited from April to October except on Tuesdays. This park opens between 10 a.m. and 12 noon and 2 p.m. to 5 p.m. although on Sundays it only opens in the afternoon. It is stressed that the cattle are wild and fierce and close approach is not possible and so binoculars and telephoto lenses are required. All the wild characteristics of the herd are retained with the king bull being chosen by the herd or more likely by his own fierce disposition. His reign continues until he can no longer hold off young rivals when he is pushed out to the fringes of the herd. Should he attempt to return he may well be bored to death. Human trespassers are at their most threatened whenever there are young calves in the herd. At this time the cows are also dangerous. Although Chillinghams are white they are not albinos because their eyes, muzzles and hooves are all black. During the cold winter of 1947 the herd almost died out and there were problems with foot and mouth in 1966 but at present some 50 animals are maintained in balance with their environment. Their wellbeing is guaranteed by the Chillingham Wild Cattle Association. Even the park itself is of interest because to hold the white cattle agricultural innovations of the 18 and 19th centuries were shunned. Without the cattle the park would be well worth a visit in its own right, as it is still medieval.

Opposite the Park is the National Trust owned Ross Castle a once vital beacon site but with the remains of an extensive earthworks. From the 1000 feet (304 m) summit there are dramatic views over to the Scottish hills, Alnwick, Holy Island and the North Sea. No wonder the site was a crucial link in the beacon chain during the wars with France. An over enthusiastic warden in 1804 lit the beacon by accident and threw the whole area into chaos. Hepburn wood just to the south of Chillingham is organised by the Forestry Commission and a series of footpaths are signed from the car park opposite the 15th century Hepburn tower, now alas just a ruin. Wooparton is situated about 8 miles to the south west of Wooler close to which was fought the battle of Hedgeley Moor in 1464. In truth this was more of a skirmish in which the Yorkist Lord Montague defeated the Lancastrian Sir Ralph Percy who was killed. The site is marked by a carved stone called the Percy Cross and reached along a footpath leading from the side of a cottage close to the Alnwick boundary sign.

Along the A697 from Wooperton there is a sign indicating Ingram and the delightfully attractive Breamish valley, which is right on the fringe of the Northumberland National Park. The Information Centre in the village has a wide ranging exhibition including the wildlife, geology and historical details of the park which stretches from the Cheviots to the Roman Wall. There are super picnic spots and a goodly number of interesting archeological sites including Greaves Ash which is about 3 miles to the west of Ingram. The settlements are reached on foot after parking on the roadside near Harside farm, the site being behind the brow of a prominent hill. The settlement dates between the last century BC and the first AD and the foundations of buildings can still be clearly seen. The double rampart which gave protection can also easily be seen. Northumberland is not well endowed with waterfalls but Linhope Spout is impressive where the Breamish crashes down 20 feet (18.3m) into a deep round pond beneath.

In the course of discovering Northumberland we enjoyed its variety — the old county has a little of everything. We hope to have proved that this is not an ugly, modern industrial county, but a beautiful, ancient, historic hard and working place. Both the wildlife and the local people are tough and forged by the harsh climate of Northumbrian winters which make the glorious days of summer all the more attractive.

Further Reading

Allsop, B. and Clark, V. (1969) *Historic Architecture of Northumberland* (Oriel Press)

Bean, D. (1971) *Tyneside — a biography* (Macmillan)

Boniface, P. and Fowler, P. (1989) *Northumberland and Newcastle upon Tyne* (Shire)

Bonser, K.J. (1970) *The Drovers* (Macmillan)

Bruce, C. (1957) *Handbook of the Roman Wall* (Reid)

Chinery, M. (1973) *A Field Guide to the Insects of Britain and Europe* (Collins)

Davies, H.A. (1974) *A Walk Along the Wall* (Weidenfeld and Nicolson)

Dixon, D.D. (1904) *Upper Coquetdale, Northumberland* (Reprint by Sandhill Press)

Dobbs, H. (1977) *Follow a wild dolphin* (Souvenir Press)

Ekwall, E. (1936, 1985) *Concise Oxford Dictionary of English Place-Names* (Oxford University Press)

Forestry Commission (1982) *The Kielder Forest* (Forestry Commission)

Frazer, C. and Emsley, K. (1978) *Northumbria* (Batsford)

Frazer, G.M. (1971) *The Steel Bonnets: the story of the Anglo-Scottish border rivers* (Barne and Jenkins)

Hunt, C.J. (1970) *The Lead Mines of the Northern Pennines* (Manchester University Press)

Hillery, C. (1990) *Northumberland National Park* (Discovery Press)

Hillery, C., Lewin, P. and Parker, M. (1990) *Northumberland Coast and Cheviot Hills* (Discovery Press)

Margary, I.D. (1973) *Roman Roads in Britain* (Baker)

Martin, M.R. (1977) *Mammals of the Seas* (Batsford)

Mee, A. (1964) *The King's England — Northumberland* (Hodder and Stoughton)

Newton, R. (1972) *The Northumberland Landscape* (Hodder and Stoughton)

Pearsall, W.H. (1958) *Mountains and Moorlands* (Collins)

Pevsner, N. and Richmond, I. (1957) *Northumberland* (Penguin)

Redfern, R.A. (1969) *Portrait of the Pennines* (Hale)

Ridley, Nancy (1965) *Portrait of Northumberland* (Hale)

Ridley, Nancy (1978) *Northumberland Then and Now* (Hale)

Ridley, Nancy (1982) *Northumberland Heritage* (Hale)

Robson, D.A. (1965) *Guide to the Geology of Northumberland and the Borders* (Natural Hist. Soc. of Northumbria)

Stamp, L.D. (1946) *Britain's Structure and Scenery* (Collins)

Stephenson, T. (1969) *The Pennine Way* (HMSO)

Turnbull, G. (1979) *Northumbria* (Ward Lock Red Guide)

Watson, G. (1974) *The Border Rivers* (Hale)

Watson, G. (1976) *Northumberland Villages* (Hale)

Wilson, R.J.A. (1975) *A Guide to the Roman Remains of Britain* (Constable)

Wright, G.N. (1981) *View of Northumbria* (David and Charles)

Wright, G.N. (1989) *The Northumbrian Uplands* (David and Charles)

Index